Prepared in cooperation with
the U.S. Agency for International Development and the U.S. Army Corps of Engineers

Groundwater-Level Trends and Forecasts, and Salinity Trends, in the Azraq, Dead Sea, Hammad, Jordan Side Valleys, Yarmouk, and Zarqa Groundwater Basins, Jordan

By Daniel J. Goode, Lisa A. Senior, Ali Subah*, and Ayman Jaber*
*Hashemite Kingdom of Jordan, Ministry of Water and Irrigation

Open-File Report 2013–1061

U.S. Department of the Interior
U.S. Geological Survey

U.S. Department of the Interior
KEN SALAZAR, Secretary

U.S. Geological Survey
Suzette M. Kimball, Acting Director

U.S. Geological Survey, Reston, Virginia: 2013

For more information on the USGS—the Federal source for science about the Earth, its natural and living resources, natural hazards, and the environment—visit *http://www.usgs.gov* or call 1–888–ASK–USGS

For an overview of USGS information products, including maps, imagery, and publications, visit *http://www.usgs.gov/pubprod*

To order this and other USGS information products, visit *http://store.usgs.gov*

Suggested citation:
Goode, D.J., Senior, L.A., Subah, Ali, and Jaber, Ayman, 2013, Groundwater-level trends and forecasts, and salinity trends, in the Azraq, Dead Sea, Hammad, Jordan Side Valleys, Yarmouk, and Zarqa groundwater basins, Jordan: U.S. Geological Survey Open-File Report 2013-1061, 80 p., available online at *http://pubs.usgs.gov/of/2013/1061/*

Contents

Figures

Tables

Conversion Factors

Multiply	By	To obtain
Length		
centimeter (cm)	0.3937	inch (in.)
millimeter (mm)	0.03937	inch (in.)
meter (m)	3.281	foot (ft)
kilometer (km)	0.6214	mile (mi)
kilometer (km)	0.5400	mile, nautical (nmi)
meter (m)	1.094	yard (yd)
Area		
square meter (m^2)	0.0002471	acre
hectare (ha)	2.471	acre
square hectometer (hm^2)	2.471	acre
square kilometer (km^2)	247.1	acre
hectare (ha)	0.003861	square mile (mi^2)
square kilometer (km^2)	0.3861	square mile (mi^2)
Volume		
liter (L)	0.2642	gallon (gal)
Mass		
gram (g)	0.03527	ounce, avoirdupois (oz)

Temperature in degrees Fahrenheit (°F) may be converted to degrees Celsius (°C) as follows:
°C=(°F-32)/1.8

Concentrations of chemical constituents in water are given either in milligrams per liter (mg/L) or micrograms per liter (µg/L).

Vertical datum and horizontal coordinate information are referenced to the Palestine 1923 / Palestine Grid. Altitude, as used in this report, refers to distance above the vertical datum.

Groundwater-Level Trends and Forecasts, and Salinity Trends, in the Azraq, Dead Sea, Hammad, Jordan Side Valleys, Yarmouk, and Zarqa Groundwater Basins, Jordan

By Daniel J. Goode, Lisa A. Senior, Ali Subah*, and Ayman Jaber*
*Hashemite Kingdom of Jordan, Ministry of Water and Irrigation

Abstract

Changes in groundwater levels and salinity in six groundwater basins in Jordan were characterized by using linear trends fit to well-monitoring data collected from 1960 to early 2011. On the basis of data for 117 wells, groundwater levels in the six basins were declining, on average about -1 meter per year (m/yr), in 2010. The highest average rate of decline, -1.9 m/yr, occurred in the Jordan Side Valleys basin, and on average no decline occurred in the Hammad basin. The highest rate of decline for an individual well was -9 m/yr. Aquifer saturated thickness, a measure of water storage, was forecast for year 2030 by using linear extrapolation of the groundwater-level trend in 2010. From 30 to 40 percent of the saturated thickness, on average, was forecast to be depleted by 2030. Five percent of the wells evaluated were forecast to have zero saturated thickness by 2030. Electrical conductivity was used as a surrogate for salinity (total dissolved solids). Salinity trends in groundwater were much more variable and less linear than groundwater-level trends. The long-term linear salinity trend at most of the 205 wells evaluated was not increasing, although salinity trends are increasing in some areas. The salinity in about 58 percent of the wells in the Amman-Zarqa basin was substantially increasing, and the salinity in Hammad basin showed a long-term increasing trend. Salinity increases were not always observed in areas with groundwater-level declines. The highest rates of salinity increase were observed in regional discharge areas near groundwater pumping centers.

Introduction

The U.S. Agency for International Development (USAID) is providing water-resources-management support to Jordan. According to USAID (2010),

> Jordan is one of the ten most water-deprived countries in the world. Lack of water will be one of the most serious challenges to Jordan's future economic growth and stability. With population expected to double by 2029, the already low availability will be halved. USAID's water portfolio activities are designed to enhance Jordan's ability to manage its water resources wisely as well as in a more integrated and efficient manner. This helps support regional stability as it prevents conflict, provides quality water for the population and improves the overall economic prospects for the country. Specific activities are initiated in partnership with the Government of Jordan (GOJ) and focus on: improving environmental protection; optimizing the availability and use of water resources; strengthening water policies and systems; and improving resource allocation.

The U.S. Geological Survey (USGS) and Hashemite Kingdom of Jordan, Ministry of Water and Irrigation (MWI) evaluated groundwater-level and salinity trends in Jordan in cooperation with USAID and the U.S. Army Corps of Engineers in order to

- Update a 2002 USGS groundwater-trends study (David W. Clark, USGS, written commun., 2002);
- Inform USAID's 5-year strategic plan,
- Evaluate trends by using all available data from MWI;
- Transfer trends estimation technology to MWI staff; and
- Provide scientific information and tools that can be used to
  - Identify a time horizon for groundwater-management planning,
  - Prioritize locations for groundwater-management actions,
  - Provide a baseline for evaluating the effects of the reduction in withdrawals planned to start in 2014,
  - Help quality assure (QA) the data,
  - Improve groundwater-model calibration,
  - Evaluate corresponding increases in groundwater-supply costs (Rosenberg and Peralta, 2011), and
  - Increase public and stakeholder awareness of groundwater trends.

Groundwater-level and electrical-conductivity (EC) data collected by the MWI, Jordan, from 1960 to early 2011 were provided in March 2011. EC commonly is used as a surrogate for salinity or total dissolved solids. Trends in groundwater levels and EC at individual wells were estimated where sufficient data were available. Groundwater-level and salinity data were evaluated for six groundwater basins in Jordan: Azraq, Dead Sea, Hammad, Jordan Side Valleys, Yarmouk, and Zarqa (fig. 1). (The Zarqa basin is also called Amman-Zarqa. The Jordan Side Valleys basin is distinct from the Jordan Valley and is also called Side Wadis or Rift Valley Side Wadis.)

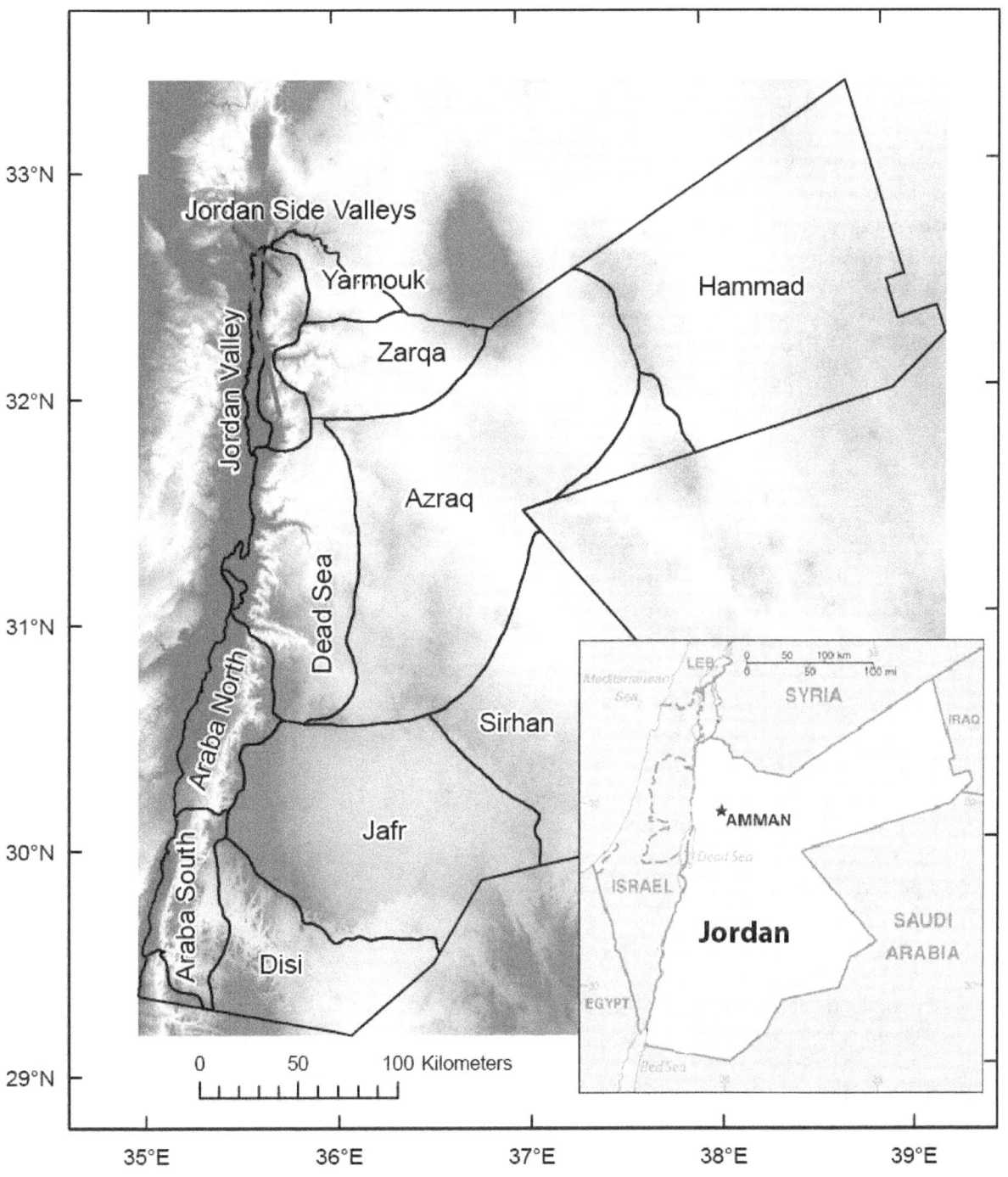

Figure 1. Areal extent of groundwater basins in Jordan. The background colors represent land-surface altitude in meters, ranging from lower than 0 (brown) to higher than 1000 (blue). Base map and all data provided by Ministry of Water and Irrigation, Jordan. Projection is Palestine 1923 Palestine Belt, Transverse Mercator. Inset map after U.S. Department of State (*www.state.gov*).

Scope

This report presents results of analyses for trends in groundwater levels and salinity (as estimated from EC data) for wells in six groundwater basins in Jordan. An overview of results for all basins is presented followed by individual presentations of trends for each of the six groundwater basins: Azraq, Dead Sea, Hammad, Jordan Side Valleys, Yarmouk, and Zarqa. Water-level data from 1968 to 2011 were analyzed for long-term trends and the trend in 2010 for wells with adequate current data. The groundwater-level trend in 2010 was used to forecast groundwater level in 2030, and saturated thickness was estimated from the groundwater level when aquifer data were available. Electrical-conductivity data from 1960 to 2011 were analyzed for long-term trends for wells with current data. A limited evaluation of the groundwater-level and EC data, regarding duration, continuity, and spatial distribution characteristics, was done as part of the trend analyses.

Setting

The main source of groundwater supply in the Azraq, Dead Sea, Hammad, Jordan Side Valleys, Yarmouk, and Zarqa basins are fractured-rock aquifers, consisting of sedimentary rocks (primarily carbonates, chert, and sandstone) and igneous rocks (primarily basalt) (table 1; see Salameh and Bannayan, 1993; Margane and others, 2001, 2002). In the Dead Sea and Jordan Side Valleys basins, unconsolidated deposits, alluvium, are also sources of groundwater supplies. The lithology of the aquifers and average annual recharge rates in groundwater basins are described by Salameh and Bannayan (1993). Additional descriptions of the aquifers in the Zarqa basin are presented by Associates in Rural Development, Inc. (2000). Of the six basins in this study, the Zarqa, Dead Sea, Jordan Side Valleys, and Yarmouk basins include high altitude areas that receive substantial recharge from local precipitation during the winter season. The Azraq basin receives less recharge but has substantial inflow from adjacent basins to the west and north as a result of recharge in those basins. The Hammad basin receives only small amounts of recharge and inflow from adjacent basins.

Table 1. Formation names, identifiers, and lithologies of major aquifers in the study area in Jordan
[After Salameh and Bannayan, 1993]

Aquifer formation name	Identifier codes	Primary lithology
Alluvium	ALL	Sand and gravel
Basalt	BA	Basalt
B4/B5	B4, B5, B4/B5	Chalk, limestone
B2/A7	A7, B2, B2/A7	Limestone
A6-A1	A2/A1, A4, A6-A1	Limestone, dolomite
Ram, Disi	RAM	Limestone, sandstone
Kurnub	K	Sandstone
Zarqa	Z	Limestone, dolomite, sandstone

Previous Investigations

Trends in groundwater levels as of 2002 were analyzed for a limited number of wells in three basins (David W. Clark, USGS, written commun., 2002). Declines in groundwater levels in the Zarqa basin are discussed in a report by Associates in Rural Development, Inc. (2000). Many publications provide water-level and salinity trends for individual wells, but a comprehensive analysis of trends has not been published to date. Some of the numerous studies of groundwater in Jordan and their findings are briefly summarized in the sections for each of the six groundwater basins discussed in this report.

Data and Methods

MWI provided groundwater-level and water-quality data from 1960 to 2010. Long-term temporal trends in groundwater levels and EC were determined by use of ordinary least squares linear regression (Helsel and Hirsch, 2002). Linear trends for water levels in 2010 were estimated graphically. Most data were used as provided. Groundwater-level trends were used to forecast aquifer saturated thickness. Wells are primarily identified by an alpha-numeric code assigned by MWI (such as F 1022) and sometimes by a well name (such as F 1022 "AZ 11").

Groundwater-Level and Salinity Data

MWI maintains a database (Water Information System (WIS)) that includes groundwater levels, aquifer-formation depths, and other information for production, monitoring, and unused wells. Over time, the amount of data on water levels in wells has increased substantially, although there has been a small decrease in the number of measurements in the database recently (2006–2010; fig. 2).

Figure 2.   Number of groundwater-level measurements for all wells in the Jordan Ministry of Water and Irrigation Water Information System database as of March 2011, by 5-year period.

Groundwater-level trends were not estimated for wells with less than six measurements separated in time, or with less than four years of data. Trends were estimated only for wells that have at least one measurement in 2009 or later. There are water-level measurements at many other wells, but only wells with data that met the criteria were analyzed for this study. Adequate water-level data were available for 117 wells in the six basins. In addition to long-term linear regression trends based on all data, trends in 2010 were estimated by graphical fit of a straight line to the most recent five years of data. Apparent data outliers, which may represent quality-assurance (QA) problems, were identified but were not corrected in all but the most obvious typographical error cases. Possible QA problems include errors in measuring, recording, or transcribing water-level or EC values. In some cases, these outliers were temporarily removed to estimate alternative trends. However, the statistics and maps developed used the data as provided.

The WIS database contains water-quality measurements, including EC, that can be used as a surrogate for salinity (dissolved salts) or total dissolved solids (TDS). Although salinity and TDS are not theoretically equivalent, practically all natural waters with high TDS also have high salinity. Salinity reflects the generation and transport of dissolved constituents in water and can be spatially variable in groundwater, depending on sample location in the flow field relative to recharge and discharge areas. Salinity generally increases substantially with depth in Jordan, as deeper waters have long residence times to accumulate dissolved salts from aquifer rocks. EC is normally measured in the field and is used to estimate salinity because measurement is simple by use of an electronic probe. In Jordan, EC is used by MWI to estimate TDS as

$$\text{TDS (micrograms per liter)} = 0.7 \, [\text{EC (in microsiemens per centimeter)}] \, .$$

Thus, the trends in EC (in microsiemens per centimeter per year (μS/cm/yr)) in this report can be converted to approximate trends in TDS [in milligrams per liter per year (mg/L/yr)] by multiplying by 0.7. Salameh (1996) identifies an EC of 1,500 μS/cm as an upper limit of freshwater suitable for all common uses.

The amount of EC data for wells in the WIS database increased after 1970, but there has been a substantial decrease in the number of measurements in the database since 2000 (fig. 3). Groundwater EC trends were estimated only for wells with data in 2009 or later, or for Azraq, Hammad, and Jordan Side Valleys basins in 2006 or later. There are EC measurement data for many other wells, but only wells with adequate current data were used for this study. Data were considered "current" if there was at least one measurement in the database during or after 2009 (or 2006). There were a few wells with current data but with less than six measurements separated over time, and only wells with six or more distinct (more than a month apart) samples were considered. A total of 205 wells were evaluated for this study. Additional wells could have been evaluated for trends if additional data in 2009 (or 2006) or later had been available.

Figure 3. Number of groundwater electrical-conductivity (EC) measurements for all wells in Jordan Ministry of Water and Irrigation Water Information System database as of March 2011, by 5-year period.

Methods for Trend Estimation

Groundwater-level trends were estimated by use of ordinary least squares linear regression to all available data. In addition, the trend in 2010 was estimated by using graphical linear fits to the last five years of data. Groundwater levels were forecast to 2030 by using the trend in 2010.

The aquifer saturated thickness in 2030 was estimated for wells for which corresponding aquifer data were available in the WIS database. The aquifer saturated thickness is a measure of the amount of water stored in the aquifer, and the saturated thickness decreases when the water level falls below the top of the aquifer. Saturated thickness forecasts were calculated as the percentage of the total aquifer thickness or, for unconfined aquifers, as the percentage of historic maximum saturated thickness, as determined from the data provided by MWI. Forecast saturated thickness was calculated as the difference between the forecast water-level altitude in 2030 and the altitude of the base of the aquifer. The percent saturated thickness forecast for 2030 was calculated as either a percent of the total aquifer thickness or the maximum historic saturated thickness. An example hydrograph for trend estimation and forecast of saturated thickness is shown in figure 4. Hydrographs for all wells evaluated are provided in an appendix for each basin.

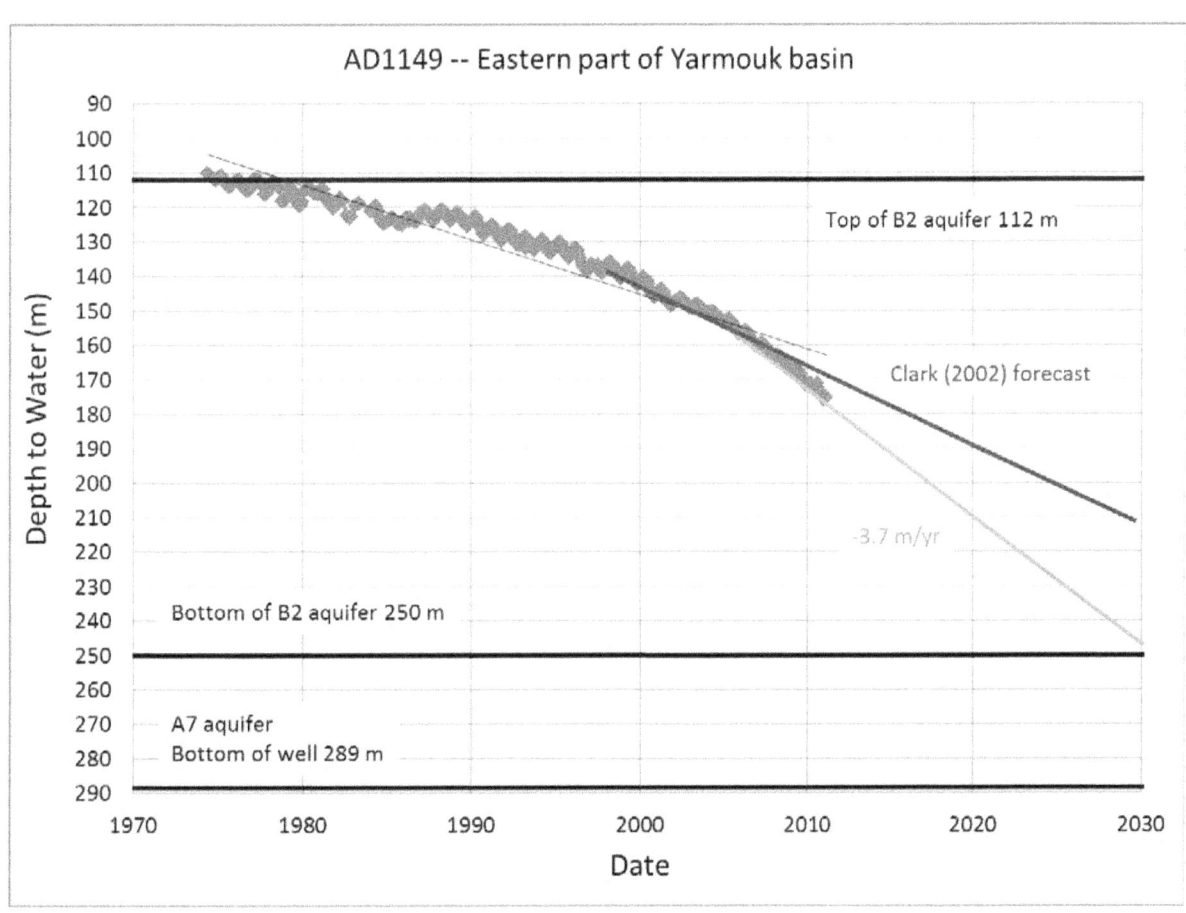

Figure 4. Groundwater hydrograph showing water levels and trend lines for well AD1149 in the eastern part of the Yarmouk groundwater basin, Jordan. (Data provided by Ministry of Water and Irrigation, Jordan; m, meters; yr, year; Clark (2002), David W. Clark, USGS, written commun., 2002)

Long-term EC trends were evaluated by use of ordinary least squares linear regression for all available data for each well. The linear trend in 2010 was not estimated, as was done for groundwater levels, because of the high variability of the EC data. Trends could possibly be computed for wells on a case by case basis, but this was not within the scope of this study. To help characterize the quality of the linear fit to the highly variable data, the coefficient of determination, R^2, is reported. An $R^2=1.0$ indicates that the EC is perfectly predicted by the linear trend over time, whereas $R^2=0.0$ indicates that none of the EC variability is explained by the trend over time. Linear fit trend lines that are flat or have a small slope generally have small values of R^2 because EC does not change over time, or the changes in EC include variations (such as those caused by measurement error, seasonality, or data gaps) that may mask any linear relation to time. Some apparent data outliers, which may represent QA problems, were identified but were not corrected in nearly all cases. In a few cases, these outliers were removed to estimate alternative trends. However, the statistics and maps developed used data as provided. Examples of graphs prepared for EC trend estimation are shown in figure 5, and examples of outliers are shown in figure 6. Graphs for all wells studied are provided in an appendix for each of the six groundwater basins.

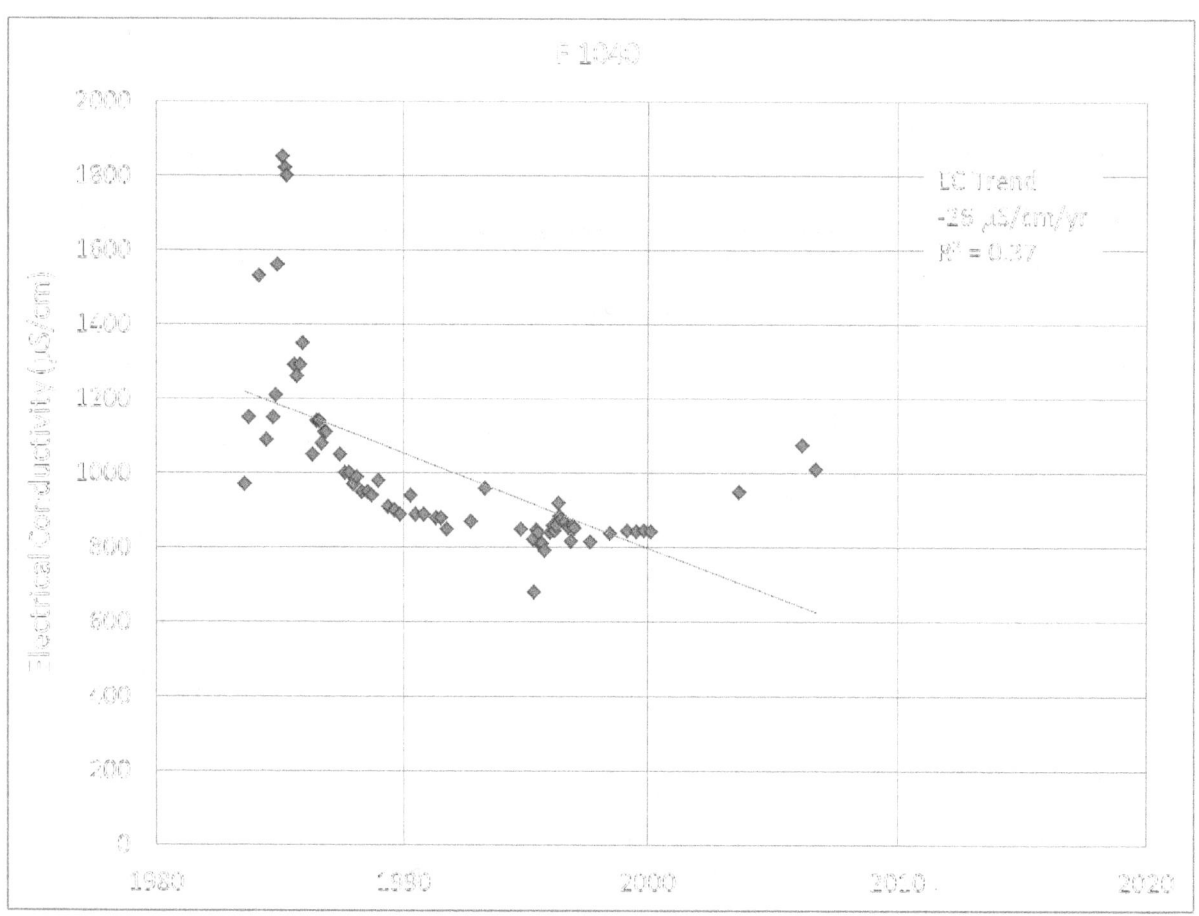

Figure 5. Groundwater electrical conductivity (EC) and trend line for well F 1040 in Azraq groundwater basin, Jordan. (Data provided by Ministry of Water and Irrigation, Jordan; µS/cm, microsiemens per centimeter; yr, year; R², coefficient of determination)

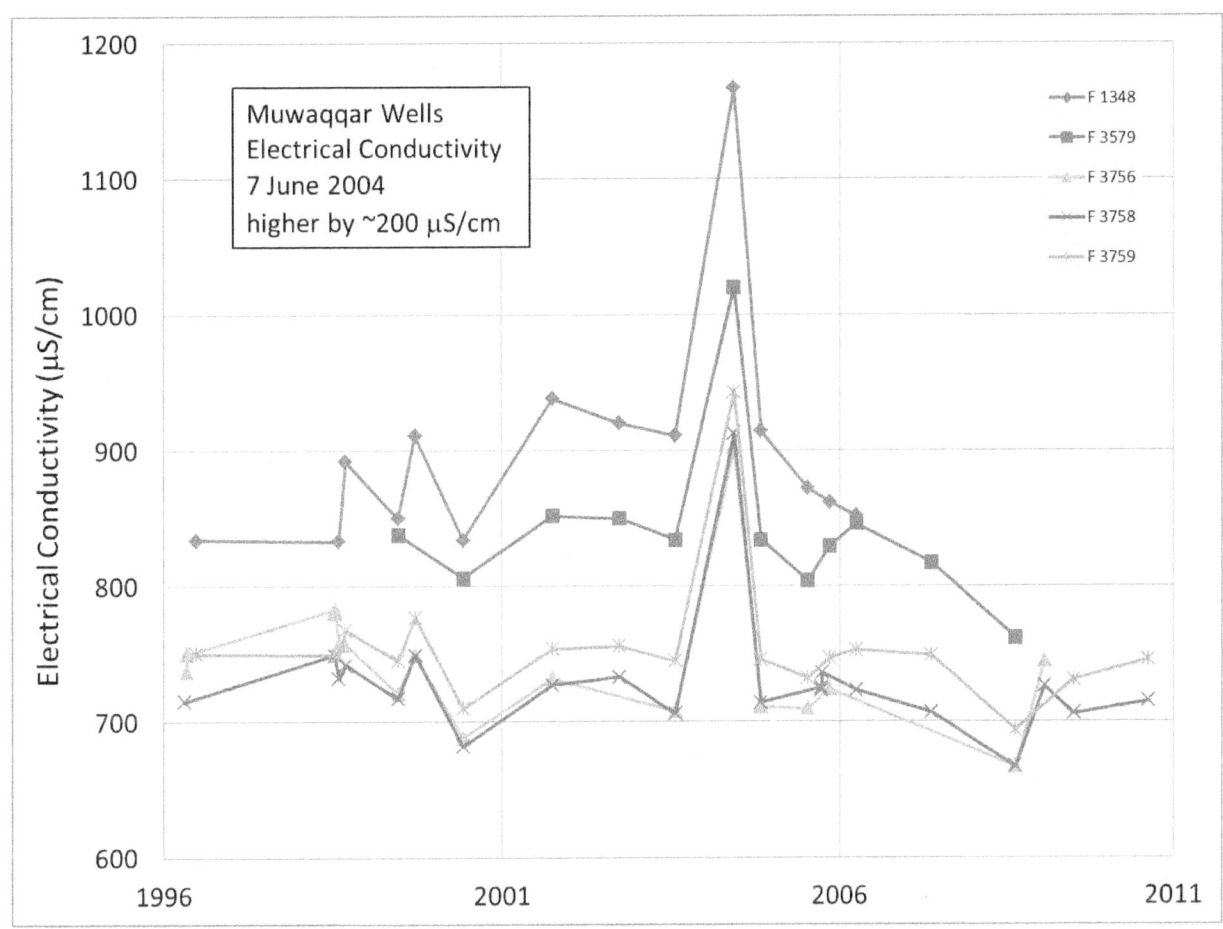

Figure 6. Groundwater electrical conductivity for Muwaqqar wells F 1348, F 3579, F 3756, F 3758, and F 3759 in the western highlands area of Azraq groundwater basin, Jordan. (Data provided by Ministry of Water and Irrigation, Jordan; μS/cm, microsiemens per centimeter)

Possible errors may affect the reliability of estimates for salinity trends in a few cases, as can be seen, for example, in EC data for Muwaqqar wells in the Azraq groundwater basin in figure 6. Apparent outliers occur for samples collected on 7 June 2004 from all five Muwaqqar wells, F 1348, F 3579, F 3756, F 3758, and F 3759, located in a pumping center in the western highlands of the Azraq groundwater basin. The EC measured for samples collected on this date is about 200 μS/cm higher than that for previous and subsequent samples at all wells (fig. 6). This may reflect a calibration problem with the analytical laboratory equipment when these samples were analyzed.

The EC variation over time can be compared to chloride (and other cations and anions) as a cross check on the data quality, although this comparison was not done systemically as part of a review of data for the trend analyses. EC and chloride are generally correlated in groundwater samples in the Azraq groundwater basin, and samples with high EC also have high chloride concentrations. However, the chloride concentrations measured for samples collected on 7 June 2004 do not show an increase in chloride concentrations similar to the EC increase for this date (fig. 7). Similarly, other cations and anions (sodium, sulfate) do not show a peak on this date. These results indicate that the EC values in the database for 7 June 2004 samples for these wells are inconsistent with other analytical results and may not reflect the geochemical conditions in this area on that date.

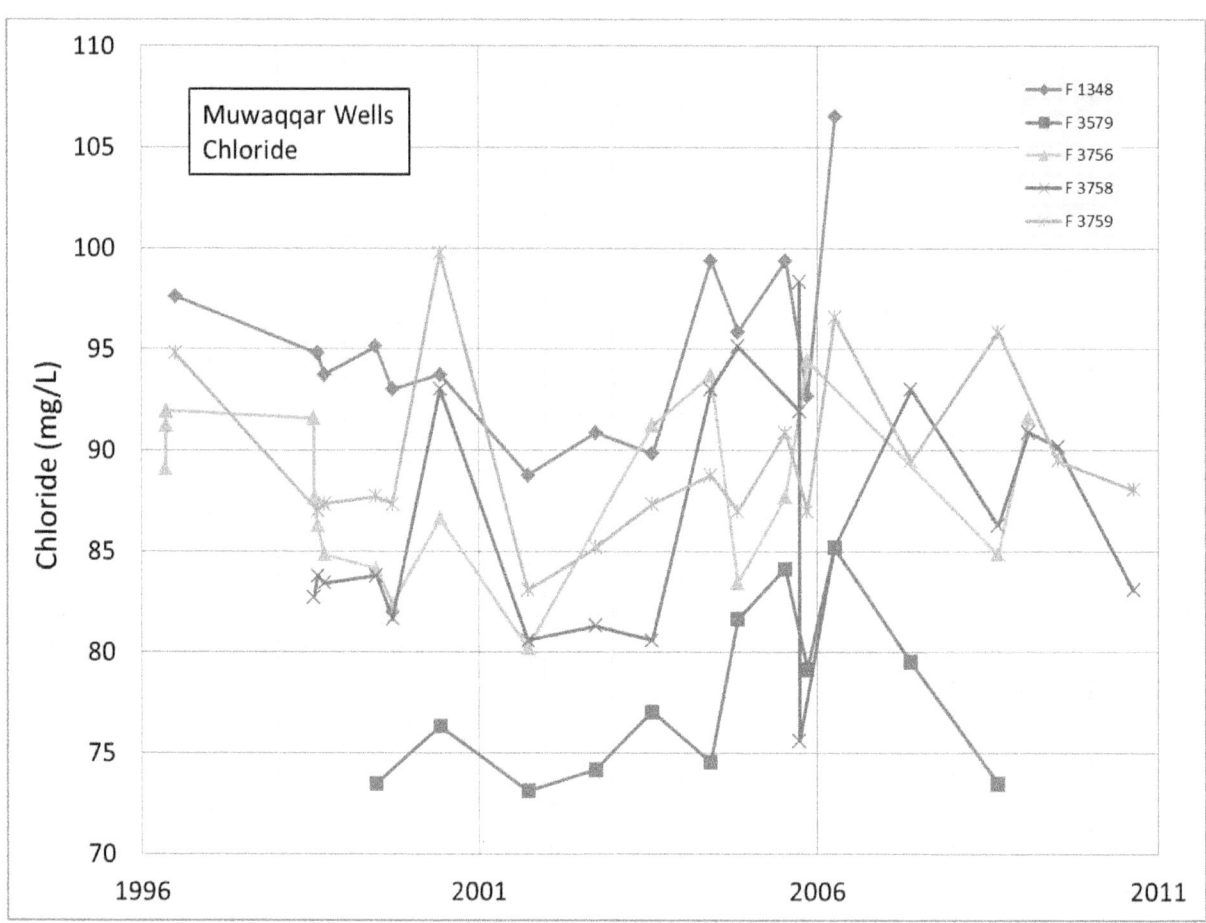

Figure 7. Groundwater chloride concentrations for Muwaqqar wells F 1348, F 3579, F 3756, F 3758, and F 3759 in the western highlands area of Azraq groundwater basin, Jordan. (Data provided by Ministry of Water and Irrigation, Jordan; mg/L, milligrams per liter)

Characteristics of Groundwater-Level and Salinity Trends

Where the data were available, long-term trends in the groundwater levels and EC were estimated for individual wells. Trends in 2010 were graphically estimated for water levels. Average trends for each of six groundwater basins were computed from the trends for individual wells in each basin. In addition, for wells where hydrogeologic information was available, the water level and trend in 2010 was used to forecast saturated thickness. Hydrographs, plots of EC measurements, and trends for all wells studied are included in the appendixes.

Groundwater-Level Trends

Most trends in groundwater levels were approximately linear over time and indicated depletion of groundwater storage. In each groundwater basin, the slope of the water-level trend lines in 2010 in many wells was steeper downward than the estimated long-term trend lines, reflecting increased rates of water-level decline. However, the rates of groundwater-level decline were not uniform across an entire groundwater basin. A basin may include wells with water levels that were relatively stable, rising slightly, or declining at differing or variable rates. These differing rates of decline indicate that groundwater-level declines varied spatially because of differences in local withdrawals, aquifer properties, and recharge rates. Examples of wells with increased and decreased rates of decline in the Azraq basin are shown in figures 8 and 9 for wells F1022 and F 1043. The rate of decline began to increase in the 1990s in monitoring well F 1022 in the Azraq oasis area (fig. 8). The rate of decline began to decrease in 2006 in well F 1043, also located in the Azraq oasis area near several wells with large withdrawals (fig. 9).

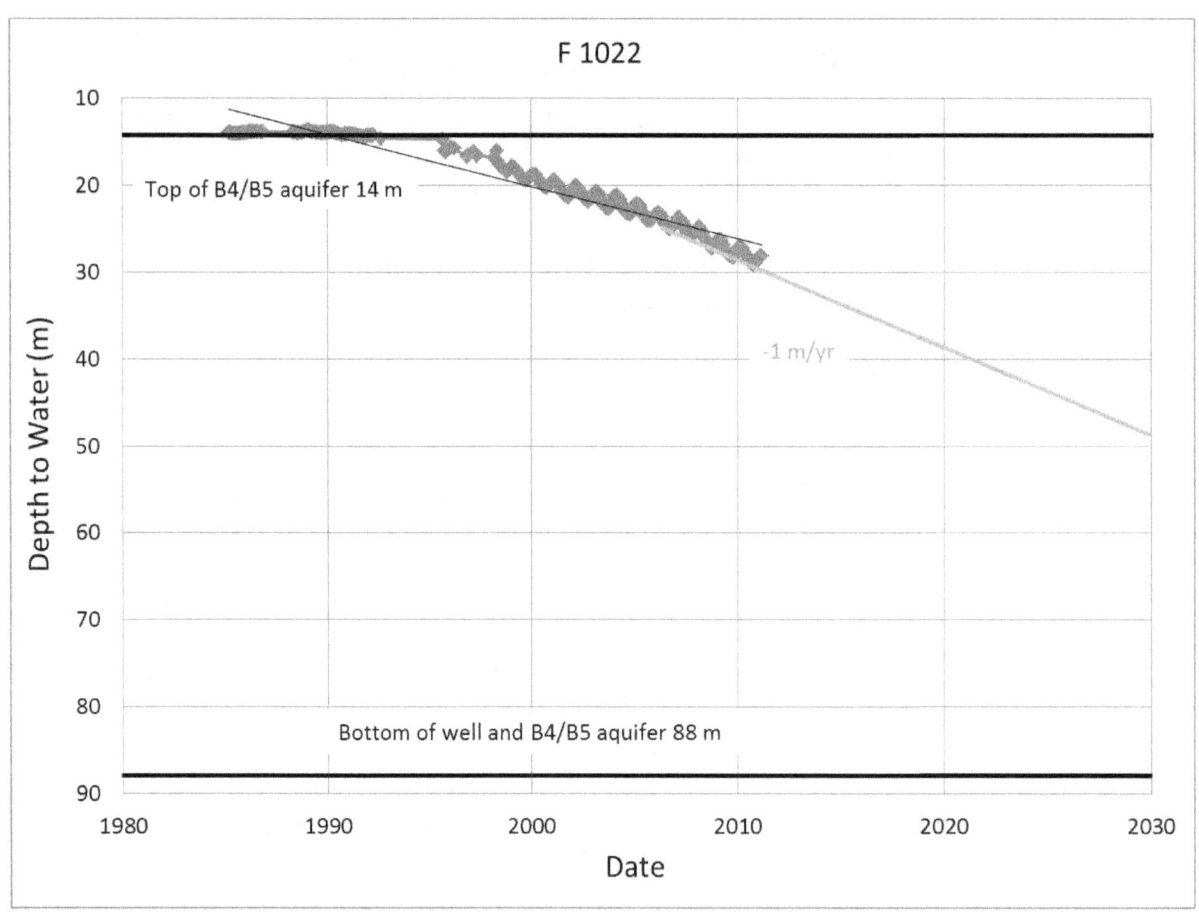

Figure 8. Groundwater hydrograph showing water levels and trend lines for well F 1022 in the Azraq groundwater basin, Jordan. (Data provided by Ministry of Water and Irrigation, Jordan; m, meters; yr, year)

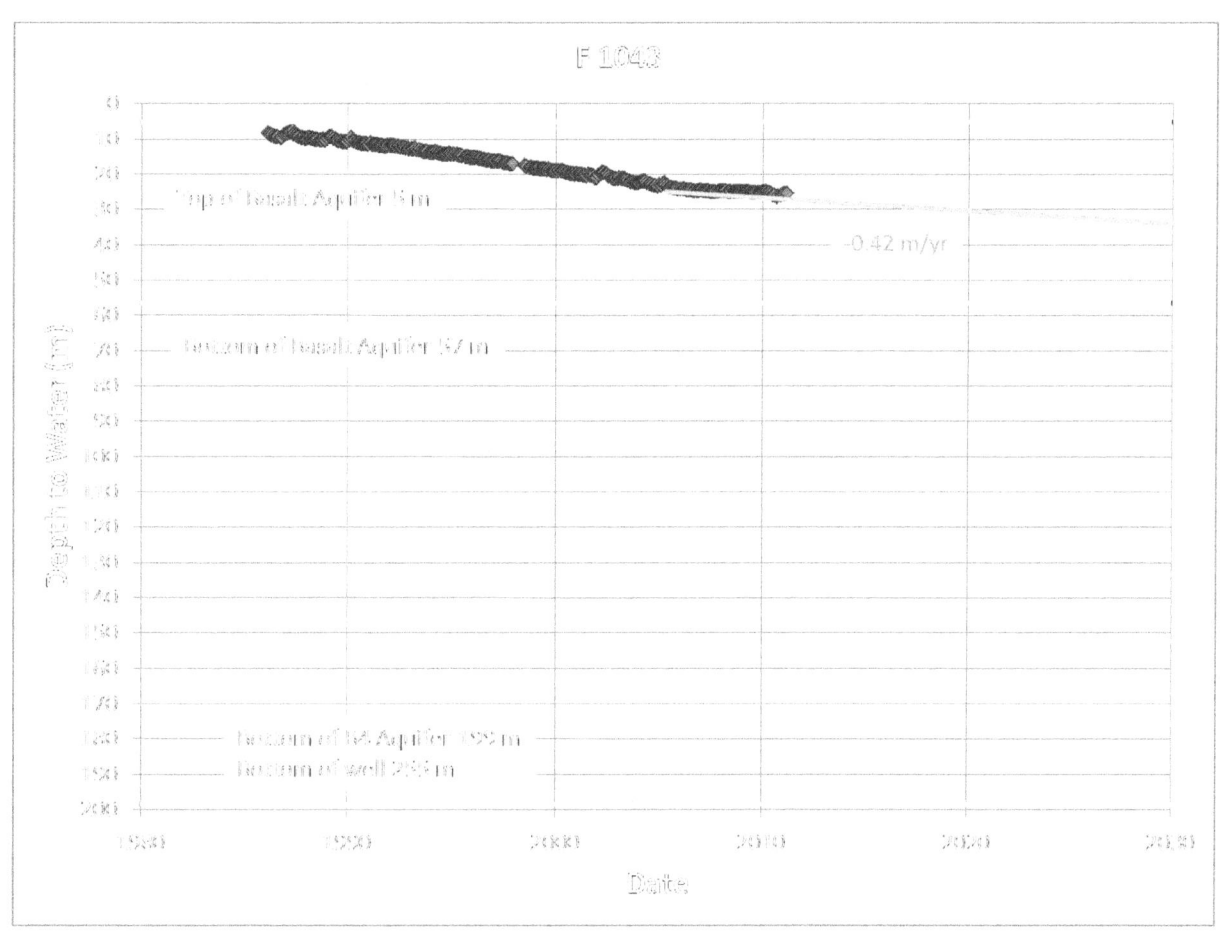

Figure 9. Groundwater hydrograph showing water levels and trend line for well F 1043 in the Azraq groundwater basin, Jordan. (Data provided by Ministry of Water and Irrigation, Jordan; m, meters; yr, year)

Seasonal fluctuations in groundwater levels reflecting seasonal changes in pumping rates and (or) recharge rates may be superimposed on overall long-term trends. For example, water levels in monitoring well F 1014 in Azraq oasis show a seasonal variation (fig. 10), but the long-term trend has been relatively constant since measurements began in 1996, declining at a rate of -0.79 meter per year (m/yr).

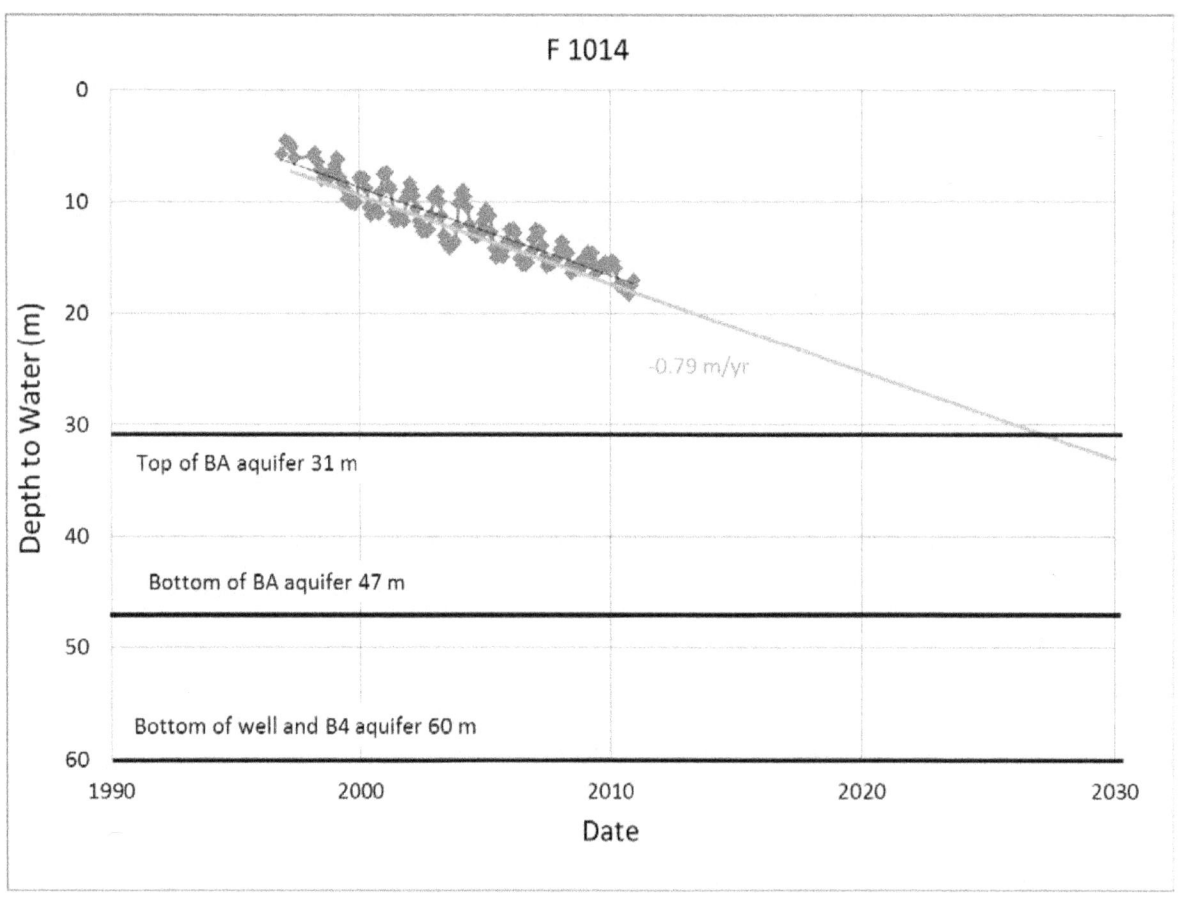

Figure 10. Groundwater hydrograph showing water levels and trend lines for well F 1014 in the Azraq groundwater basin, Jordan. (Data provided by Ministry of Water and Irrigation, Jordan; m, meters; yr, year)

Salinity Trends

Trends in salinity estimated from EC generally were not as linear over time as trends in groundwater levels, and missing EC data affected the ability to determine trends. The EC trend estimates are considered highly uncertain because of the range in strengths of linear trend fits to the data, as measured by R^2. The uncertainty includes possible cases where a small R^2 could indicate no change (slope of trend line near 0) instead of a poor fit resulting from the small number of EC measurements, which was the situation for many locations. The variability of EC is a result of various processes, such as the amounts of water supplied by aquifers with different chemical characteristics or loadings from land-use activities through recharge. The change or lack of change in EC values over time could be analyzed to infer possible causes of changes in observed values at individual wells or groups of wells, but that analysis is beyond the scope of this report.

Examples of non-linear changes in EC include a downward curving trend for F 1040 (fig. 5) and two periods with abruptly different trends for well F 1042 (fig. 11). An example of EC data that exhibits no trend (slope is near 0) is shown for well F 1033 (fig. 12).

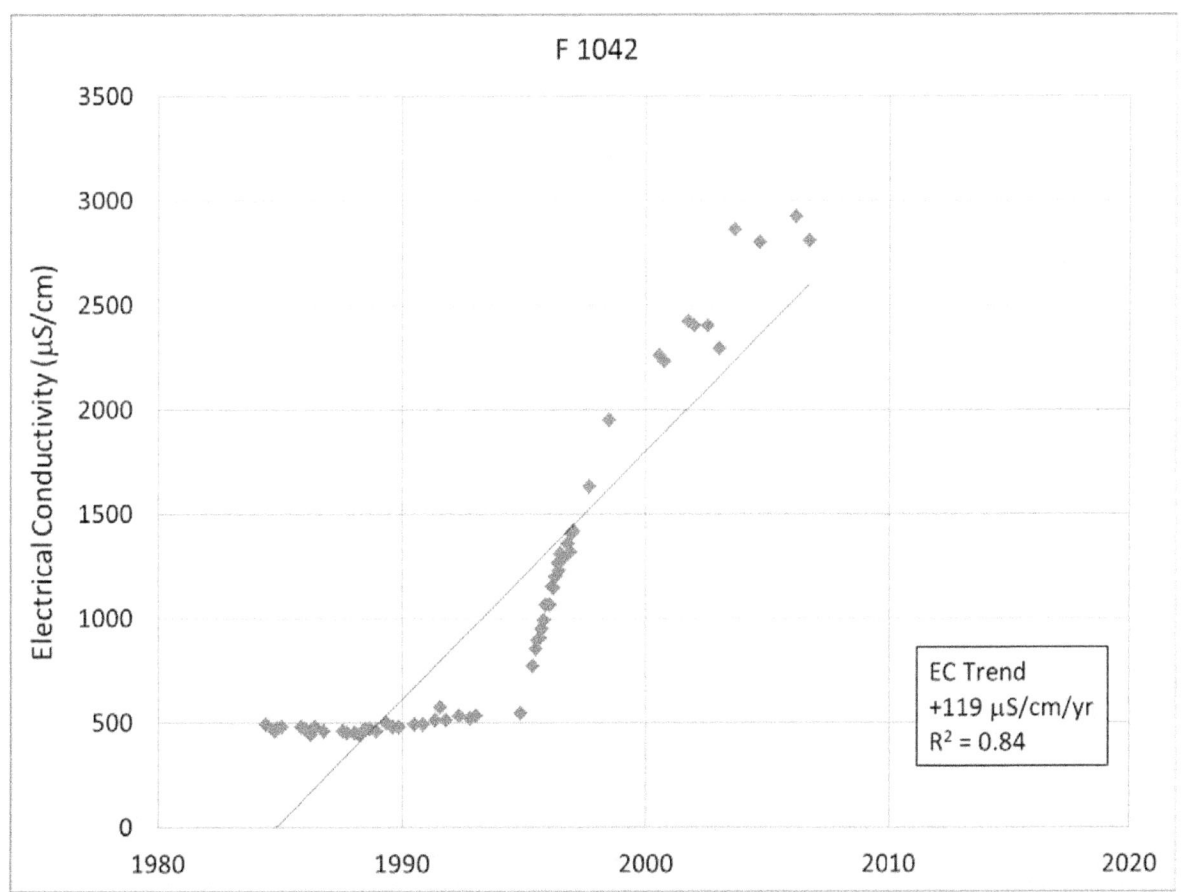

Figure 11. Groundwater electrical conductivity (EC) and trend line for well F 1042 in the AWSA well field in the Azraq groundwater basin, Jordan. (Data provided by Ministry of Water and Irrigation, Jordan; μS/cm, microsiemens per centimeter; yr, year; R^2, coefficient of determination).

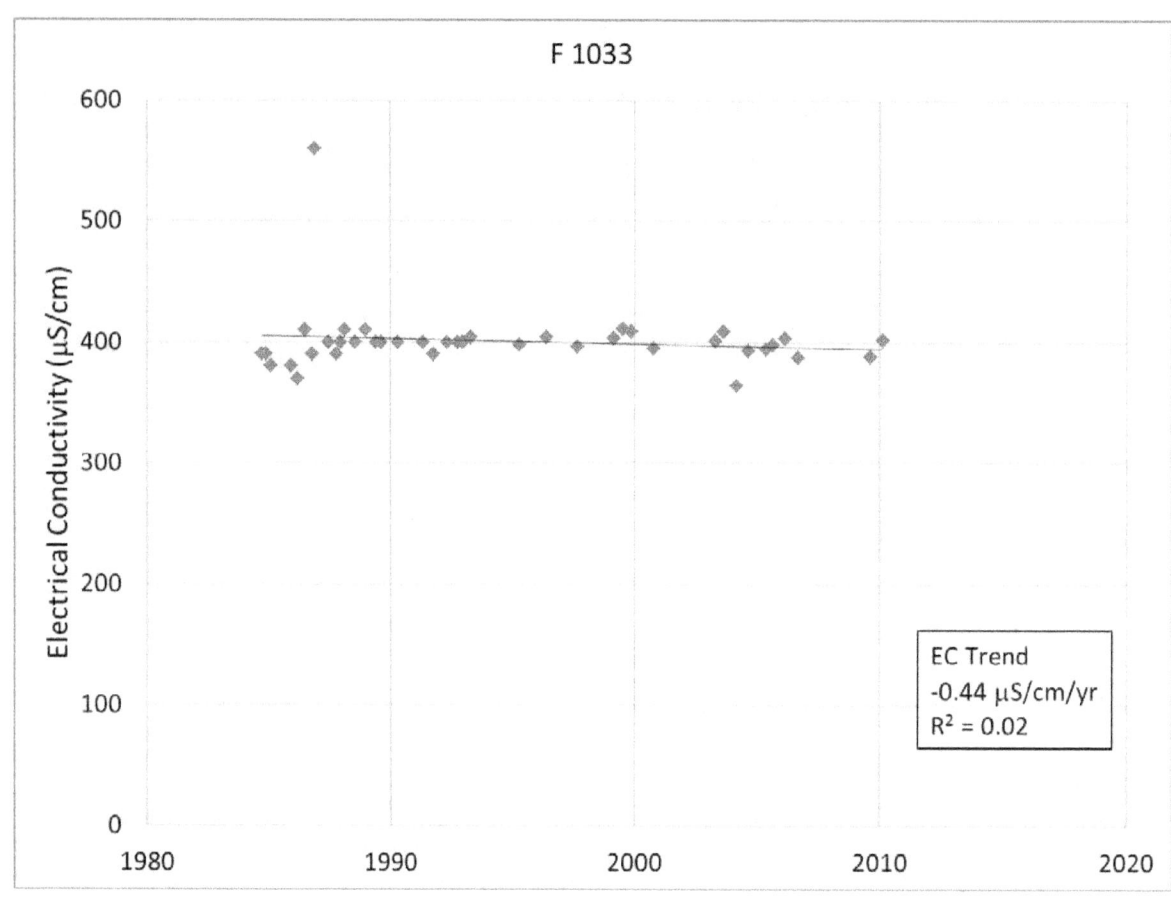

Figure 12. Groundwater electrical conductivity (EC) and trend line for well F 1033 in the Azraq groundwater basin, Jordan. (Data provided by Ministry of Water and Irrigation, Jordan; μS/cm, microsiemens per centimeter; yr, year; R^2, coefficient of determination)

Azraq Groundwater Basin

Groundwater flow in the Azraq basin is generally from highland recharge areas in the west and north towards the central oasis area where groundwater has historically discharged by evapotranspiration from the oasis wetlands (Salameh, 1996). The decline of the groundwater levels as a result of over-pumping in the Azraq basin, and the drying up of the oasis wetlands, are well known and have been documented by numerous reports. For example, El-Naqa and others (2007) show groundwater-level hydrographs at two Azraq wells and describe correlated changes in water quality. Dotteridge and Abu Jaber (1999) summarize groundwater over-pumping and report flow-model forecasts of future declines in the Azraq basin:

> ... results suggest that, if abstraction continues at present rates, the springs will remain dry and water levels will fall by an average of 0.7 m yr^{-1} at Azraq, but the rate of decline will increase with time as the storage in the aquifer is depleted. As water levels fall, this will cause a continual reduction in the saturated thickness of the aquifer, which is less than 50 m thick in the center of the basin. Consequently, pumping costs will increase and well yields may reduce, particularly in the AWSA well field. It is predicted that the problems will increase with time, until large-scale abstraction becomes impossible from the central part of the basin, after approximately 40 years.

Salinization of groundwater in the Azraq groundwater basin also has been studied by numerous authors. Salameh (1996) described the Azraq basin hydrogeology and water resources, and summarized the distribution and changes of groundwater salinity caused by groundwater withdrawals and artificial recharge in the oasis area. El-Naqa and others (2007; see also Al-Momani and others, 2006) examined geochemical conditions and isotope ratios and found that upward flow resulting from over-pumping in the AWSA well field area and dissolution of salts in the rock matrix in underlying lower-permeability carbonate rocks were the source of salinization of AWSA wells F 1028, F 1039, and F 1042. Kaudse and Aeschbach-Hertig (2011) corroborated this finding with dissolved-gas data. Al-Momani and others (2006) reported upward salinity trends in 3 of 15 wells studied. Abu-El-Sha'r and Hatamleh (2007) simulated groundwater flow and EC transport (as a surrogate for salinity) under different management scenarios and found that EC was much less sensitive than water levels to changes in withdrawals or recharge.

Groundwater Levels

Analyses of trends for this study show that groundwater levels were declining in all areas of the Azraq groundwater basin. Of the 21 wells studied,15 monitoring wells had adequate data for analysis of water-level trends in 2010. Groundwater levels were declining at all 15 monitoring wells in the basin (table 2; fig. 13). The rate of groundwater-level decline for the 2010 data ranged from -0.14 to -2.3 m/yr. The average water-level trend in 2010 at monitoring wells in the Azraq groundwater basin was -0.8 m/yr. Four wells showed moderate to substantial declines in water levels prior to 2007 (table 2) but current data (2009 or later) were not in the database. Thus, the trend at these wells in 2010 could not be evaluated without additional measurements. Two other wells had upward water-level trends of +0.42 and +0.91 m/yr from 1999 through 2007 and 2008, respectively (table 2), but current data were not available for these wells in the WIS database. All groundwater-level trend graphs are provided in Appendix A.

Table 2. Groundwater-level trends and forecast saturated aquifer thicknesses at selected wells in the Azraq groundwater basin, Jordan. [*Link*]

In general, groundwater levels were declining most rapidly in areas of high groundwater withdrawals. Most monitoring wells are concentrated around the Azraq oasis where many withdrawal wells are located. The highest rate of decline (-2.3 m/yr) is at a well (F 3755) in the highlands, an area of concentrated withdrawals (fig. 13). The smallest rate of decline (-0.14 m/yr in well F 1286) is in an area with little pumping. Water-level measurements were not available in large areas of the Azraq basin, so the groundwater-level trends in these areas were unknown.

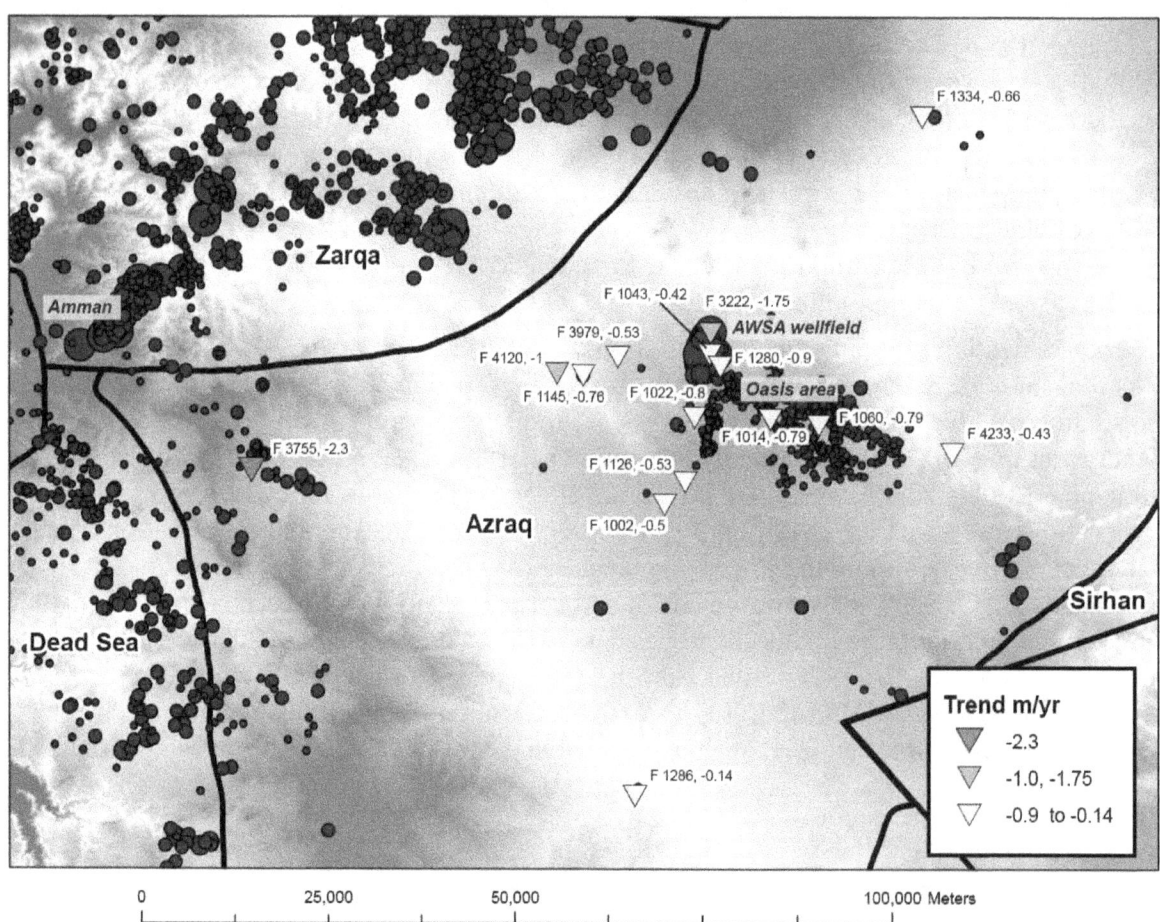

Figure 13. Trends in groundwater levels at selected wells in the Azraq groundwater basin, Jordan. The background colors represent land-surface altitude in meters, ranging from lower than 400 (brown) to higher than 900 (blue). The groundwater-level trend in 2010, in meters per year, is shown for all wells with data in 2009 or later. Negative trends indicate declining water levels. The dark-blue dots are production wells, and the size of the dot represents the annual withdrawal from each well in 2009. (Data provided by Ministry of Water and Irrigation, Jordan; m/yr, meters per year)

Rates of groundwater-level decline were essentially unchanged when comparing trends from historic data to trends in 2010 for 5 of the 15 wells studied: F 1014, F 1060, F 1145, F

3979, and F 4233 (table 2). Downward water-level trends recently steepened in seven wells. Relative to long-term trends, rates of decline in 2010 increased by more than -0.1 m/yr in four wells: F 1022, F 1126, F 1280, and F 3222. The rate of water-level decline decreased recently in three wells: F 1043, F 1334, and F 3755 (table 2). Some wells in the Azraq basin, for example F 1022, had seasonal fluctuations in water levels that were superimposed on long-term trends.

By using aquifer-thickness and well-depth data, where available, the average saturated thickness at the well locations in the Azraq basin was forecast for 2030 to be 69 percent of the initial or total saturated thickness (table 2). The forecast saturated thickness in 2030 ranged from 14 to 100 percent at the well locations (table 2; fig. 14).

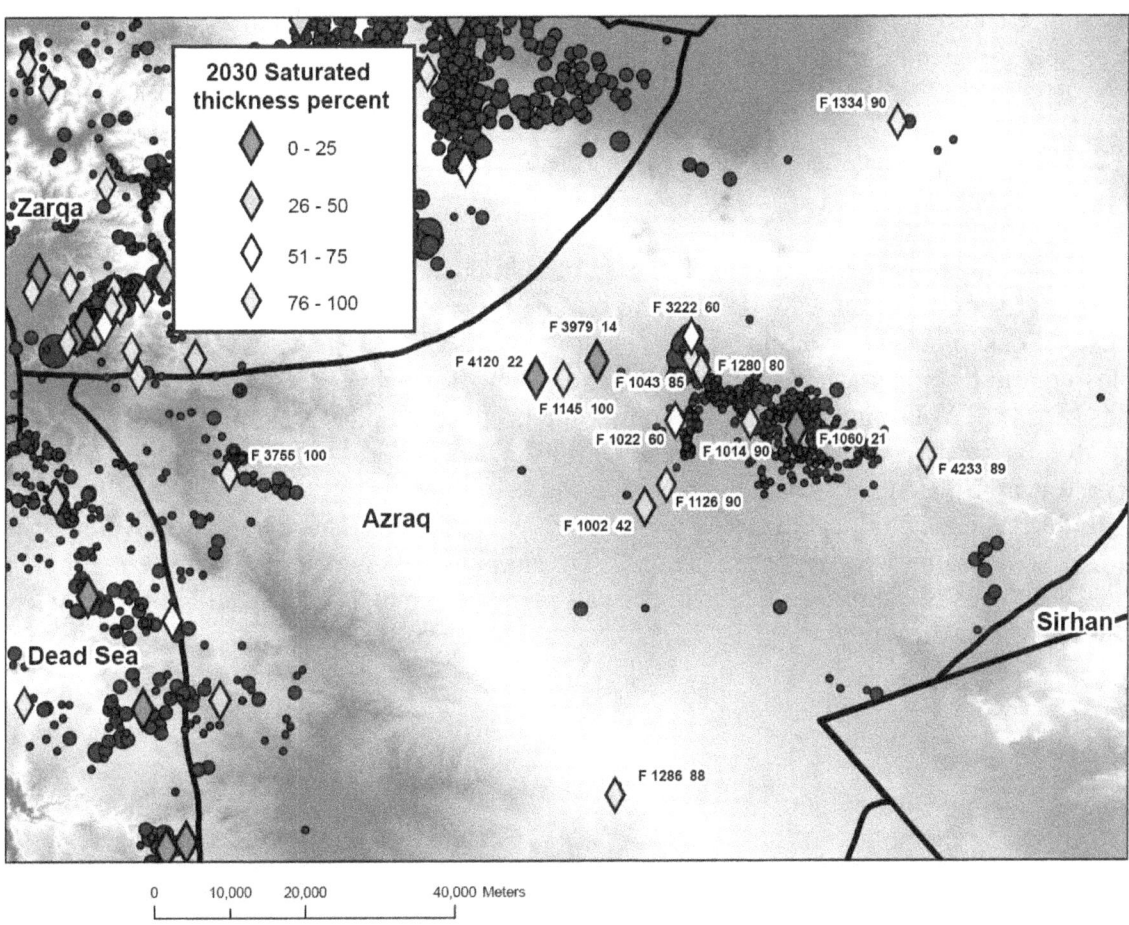

Figure 14.   Forecast saturated aquifer thickness in 2030 at selected wells in the Azraq groundwater basin, Jordan. The background colors represent land-surface altitude in meters, ranging from lower than 400 (brown) to higher than 900 (blue). The dark-blue dots are production wells, and the size of the dot represents the annual withdrawal from each well in 2009. (Data provided by Ministry of Water and Irrigation, Jordan)

Salinity

Trends in groundwater salinity estimated for this study by use of linear regression for EC data where variable in the Azraq groundwater basin (table 3). The R^2 ranged from 0.01 to 0.93 for the 25 wells studied. In general, the trend estimates are considered highly uncertain because of the variable strength of linear fits to the data, as measured by R^2, and the small number of EC measurements at many locations (table 3). Only 12 wells in the database had data for 2009 or later. The criterion for selecting wells with current data was changed to 2006 or later, in order that more wells, a total of 25, could be used for the trend analysis. Of these 25 wells, 9 had increasing groundwater EC trends , 12 had flat trends (from -5 to +5 µS/cm/yr), and 4 had decreasing trends (table 3). The quality of the fit of the linear trend over time and the scatter of data around this trend line are graphically illustrated for all wells studied (Appendix A).

Table 3. Groundwater electrical-conductivity trends at selected wells in the Azraq groundwater basin, Jordan. [*Link*]

The trends were relatively flat in the western highlands of the Azraq basin. A sharp increase in EC occurred at many wells in the Azraq oasis area, AWSA well field, and other low-lying locations in the center of the basin. Basin-wide, EC was increasing most rapidly in wells at the lower altitudes in the basin (fig. 15). However, some nearby wells had flat or decreasing EC trends (fig. 16). Wells outside major pumping centers (for example, the AWSA well field) generally had relatively stable or decreasing salinity, whereas wells in major pumping centers had both increasing and decreasing trends. The causes of the variability in trends, and current EC, are likely related to local hydrogeologic and flow conditions. The Azraq basin wells with the highest rates of salinity increases are generally in pumping centers near the basin center, but some are in areas of the basin where withdrawals were moderate, such as well F1063 in the southeastern part of Azraq basin (fig. 15).

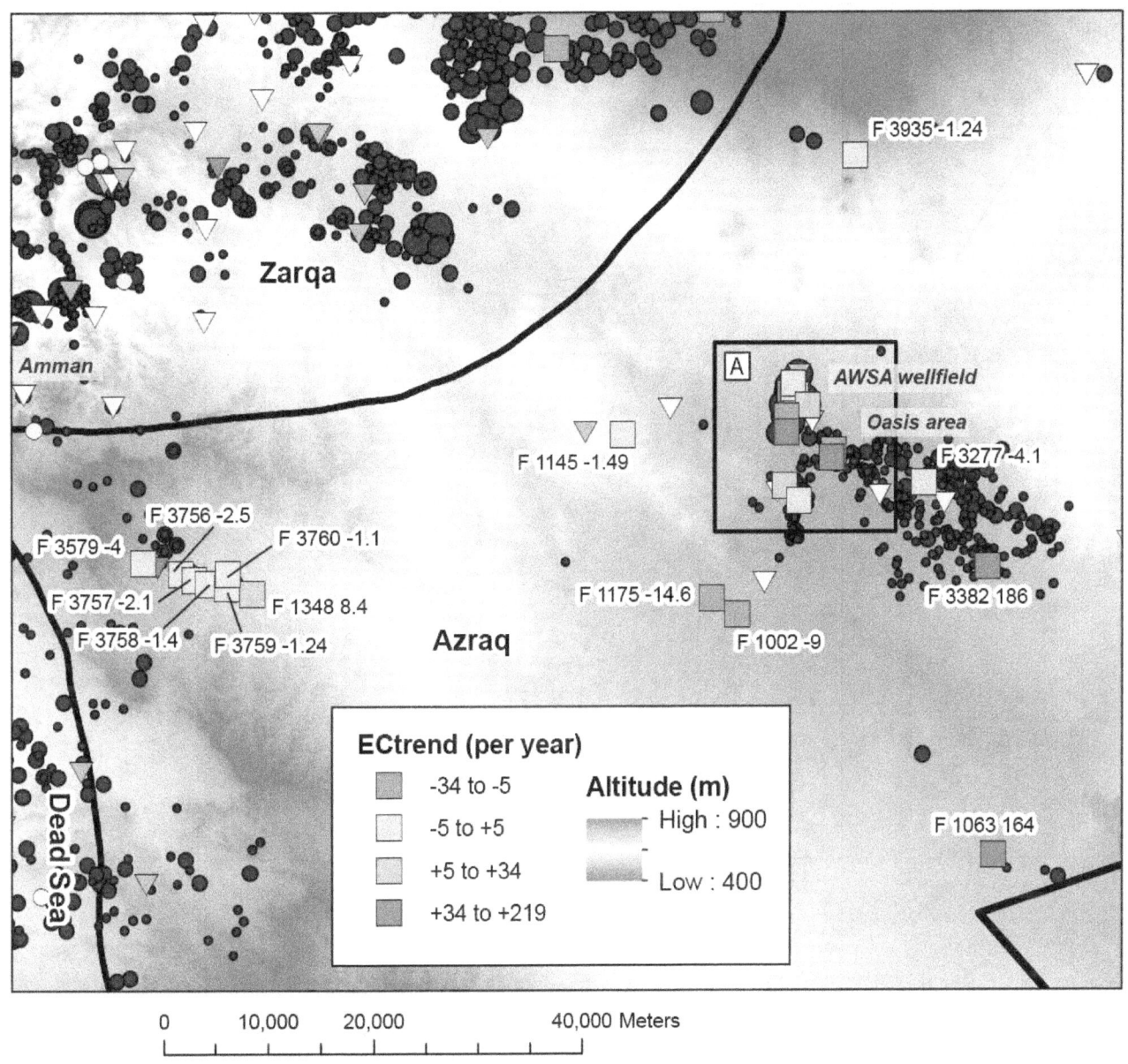

Figure 15. Trends in groundwater electrical conductivity (EC) at selected wells in the Azraq groundwater basin, Jordan. Details in area of AWSA well field in box (A) are shown in Figure 16. The background colors represent land-surface altitude in meters. The long-term EC trend, in microsiemens per centimeter per year, is shown for all wells with data in 2006 or later. Negative trends indicate decreasing EC. Triangles represent the current groundwater-level trends (see fig. 13). The dark-blue dots are production wells, and the size of the dot represents the annual withdrawal from each well in 2009. (Data provided by Ministry of Water and Irrigation, Jordan; m, meters)

23

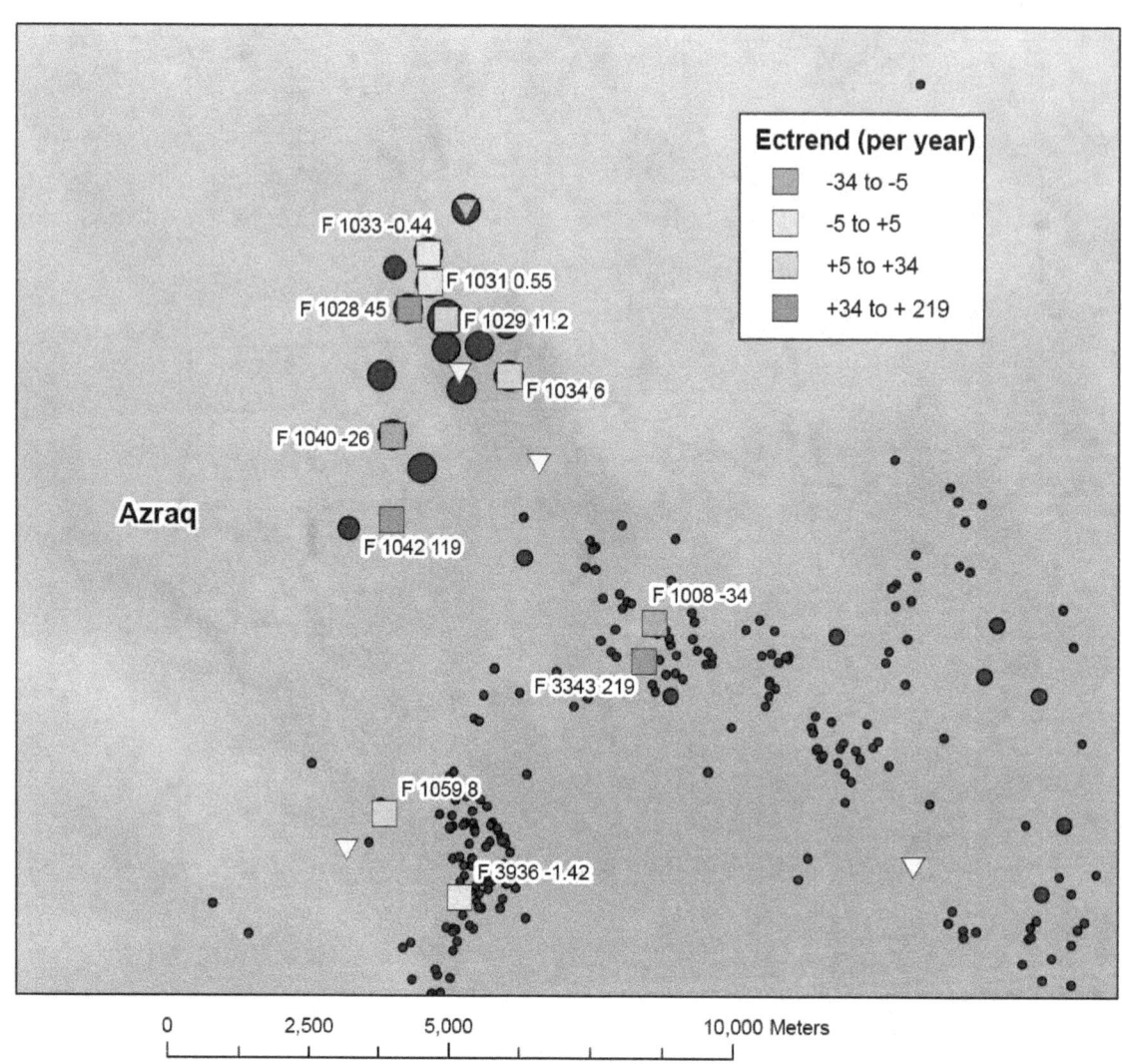

Figure 16. Details of trends in groundwater electrical conductivity (EC) at selected wells in the area of AWSA well field in the Azraq groundwater basin, Jordan. Location shown in figure 15. The background colors represent land-surface altitude in meters, ranging from lower than 400 (brown) to higher than 900 (blue). The long-term EC trend, in microsiemens per centimeter per year, is shown for all wells with data in 2006 or later. Negative trends indicate decreasing EC. Triangles represent the current groundwater-level trend (see fig. 13). The dark-blue dots are production wells, and the size of the dot represents the annual withdrawal from each well in 2009. (Data provided by Ministry of Water and Irrigation, Jordan)

Dead Sea Groundwater Basin

The Dead Sea groundwater basin is located along the eastern shore of the Dead Sea (see fig. 1). Groundwater recharge occurs primarily in the eastern highland area of the basin in the winter, and recharge is highest in the northern highlands as a result of the regional precipitation pattern (Salameh and Bannayan, 1993). Groundwater discharges to many at mid- and low-altitude springs towards the western part of the basin, and the ultimate discharge is to the Dead Sea, a terminal hyper-saline lake. The lowering of the Dead Sea water level during the last several decades as a result of capturing of flood runoff and over-pumping of groundwater from the basin is well known (Salameh and El-Naser, 2009). Major intermittent streams in the basin include, in the northern part, Wadi Heedan and Wadi Wala; in the central part, Wadi Mujib; and, in the southern part, Wadi Al Hasa (fig. 17). Margane and others (2009a) describe the hydrology of the Wadi Heedan/Wadi Wala area, including the distribution of groundwater EC. Margane and others (2008, 2010) describe the hydrology and hydrogeology of Wadi Mujib basin. Several major pumping centers for municipal supply are located in the high-altitude recharge areas of the Dead Sea basin. In addition, the Wadi Mujib dam (not shown) provides the primary brackish raw water for the Zara-Ma'een desalination plant, which provides freshwater for Amman and other areas.

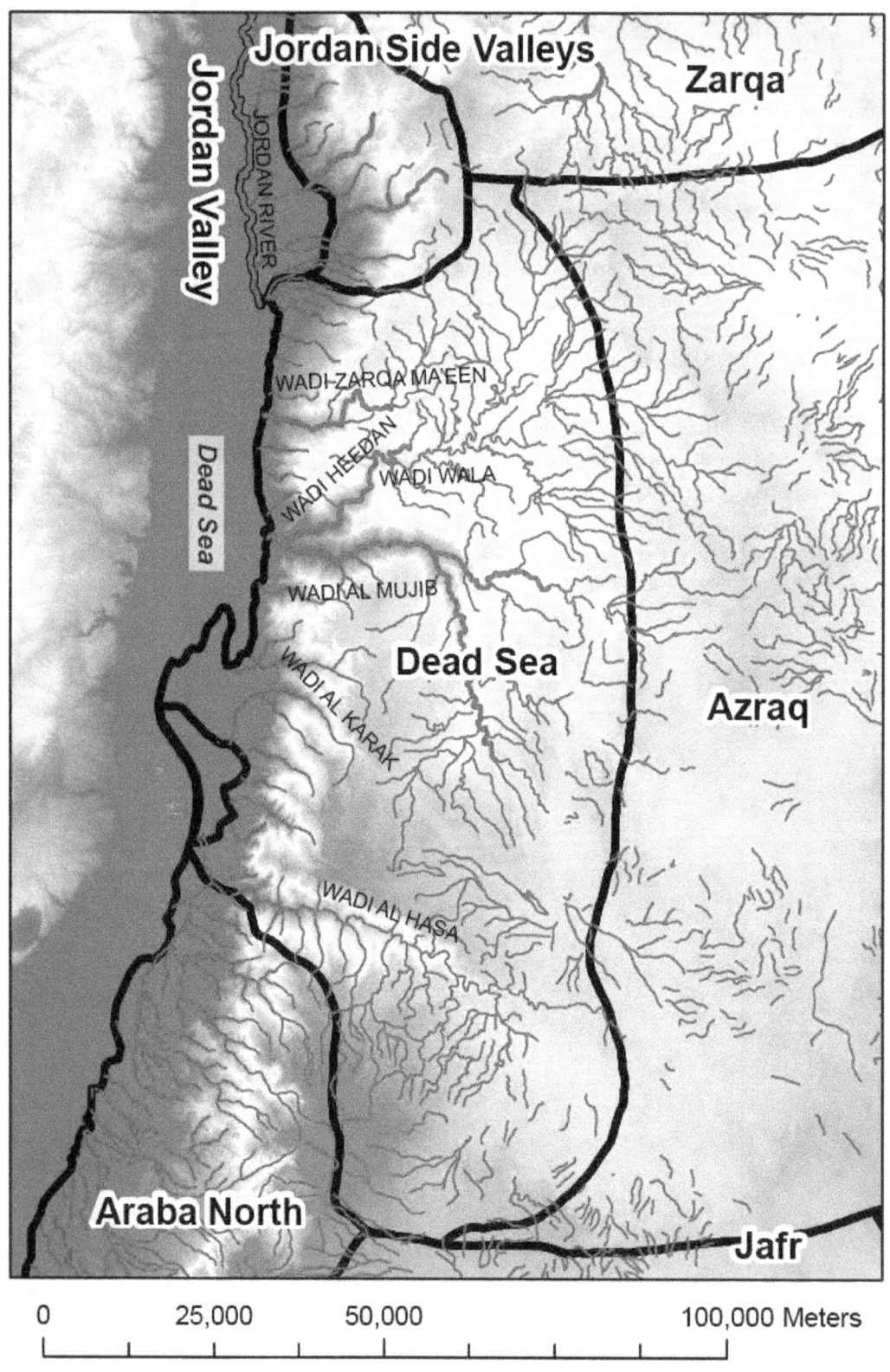

Figure 17. Dead Sea groundwater basin, Jordan. The background colors represent land-surface altitude in meters, ranging from -461 (brown) to 2796 (blue). Blue lines indicate major (thick) and minor (thin) stream channels. (Data provided by Ministry of Water and Irrigation, Jordan)

Groundwater Levels

Groundwater levels were declining in most wells in the Dead Sea groundwater basin. A total of 30 of 34 monitoring wells had adequate data in the database for use in the analysis of water-level trends in 2010. Of these, groundwater levels were declining at 21 wells, were flat at 6 wells, and rising at 3 wells (table 4). The maximum rate of groundwater-level decline was -9 m/yr, and the maximum rate of groundwater-level increase was 0.26 m/yr. The trend was was downward by more than -1 m/yr for 8 of 30 wells (fig. 18). All groundwater-level trend graphs are provided in Appendix B.

Table 4. Groundwater- level trends and forecast saturated aquifer thicknesses at selected wells in the Dead Sea groundwater basin, Jordan. [*Link*]

Figure 18. Histogram of groundwater-levels trends in 2010 for the Dead Sea groundwater basin, Jordan. The groundwater-level trend, in meters per year, is shown for all wells with data in 2009 or later. Negative trends indicate declining water level. Note that the histogram bins are nonuniform. (Data provided by Ministry of Water and Irrigation, Jordan)

Greater rates of groundwater-level decline were identified in the northern and central areas of the Dead Sea groundwater basin than in the southern area. The northern part of the Dead Sea groundwater basin includes the major intermittent streams Wadi Heedan and Wadi Wala, as well as areas that contribute base flow to Wadi Zarqa Ma'een and springs near the Dead Sea. Of the 13 wells in the northern area with sufficient data, 8 had downward trends, 1 had an upward trend, and 4 had flat trends (fig. 19). In general, groundwater levels were declining most rapidly in the higher altitudes to the east, which was the area of highest precipitation and groundwater recharge. This was also the area with the largest groundwater withdrawals. A high rate of water-level decline, -5 m/yr, was observed during 2007 at well CD1136 (Appendix B); however, the current trend was flat at this well, perhaps because of reductions in nearby pumping rates. The last water-level measurement in the database was made in February 2009. The groundwater-level trend was rising (+0.2 m/yr) near the Wadi Wala dam likely because of increased local groundwater recharge.

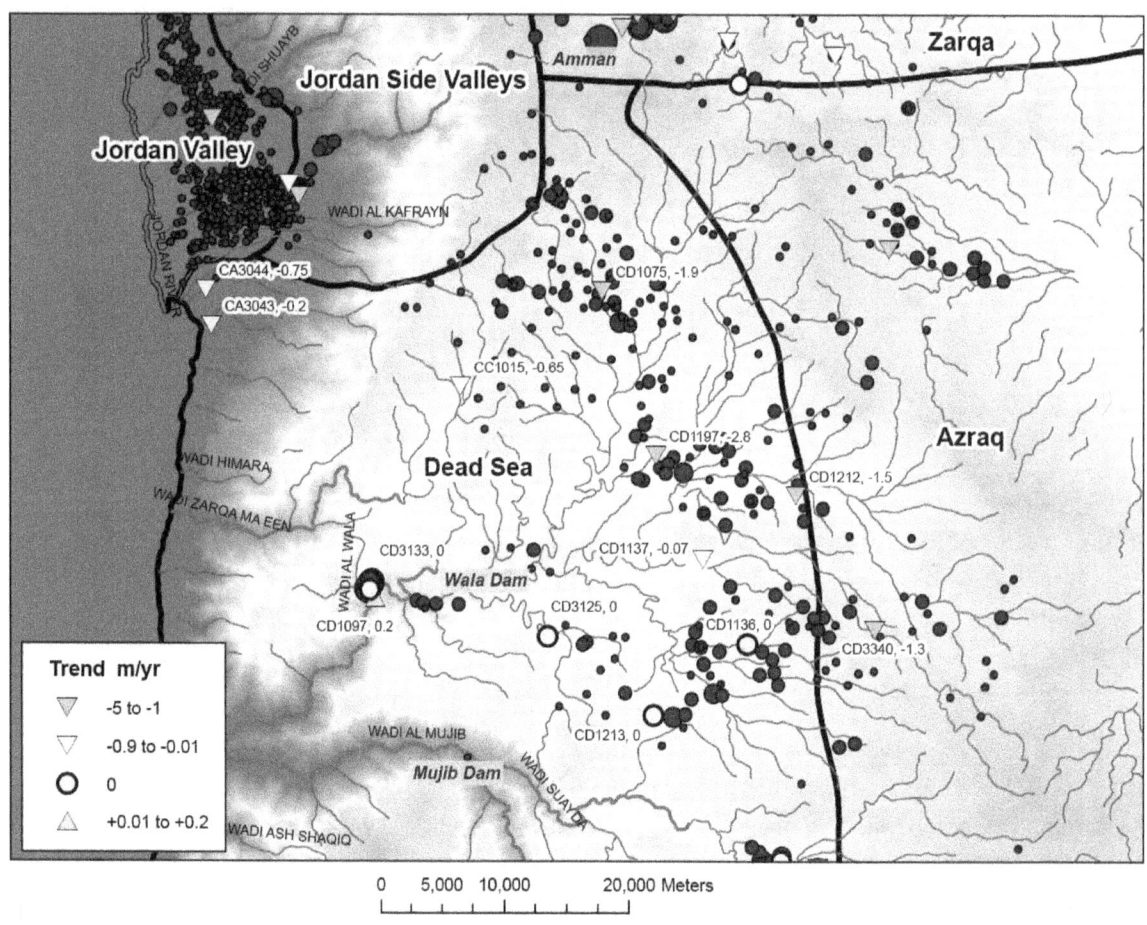

Figure 19. Trends in groundwater levels at selected wells in the northern Dead Sea groundwater basin, Jordan. The background colors represent land-surface altitude in meters, ranging from -461 (brown) to 2796 (blue). The groundwater-level trend in 2010, in meters per year, is shown for all wells with data in 2009 or later. Negative trends indicate declining water levels. The dark-blue dots are production wells, and the size of the dot represents the annual withdrawal from each well in 2009. Blue lines are streams. (Data provided by Ministry of Water and Irrigation, Jordan; m/yr, meters per year)

The central part of the Dead Sea groundwater basin (fig. 20) includes the major intermittent stream Wadi Al Mujib; the base flow and flood runoff of Wadi Al Mujib are captured by a dam and used for water supply. Of the 11 groundwater wells with sufficient data, 7 had downward trends, 2 had flat trends, and 2 had upward trends (fig. 20). In general, groundwater levels were declining most rapidly in the higher altitudes to the east, which was the area of highest precipitation and groundwater recharge. This was also the area with the largest groundwater withdrawals. Major pumping centers in the basin were at Swaqah, Qatrana, Lajjun, and Sultani. The highest rate of water-level decline was -9 m/yr in well CD1010, which may be a production well, at the Swaqah well field. Small upward trends were observed at two monitoring wells near the Dead Sea in areas with small or no withdrawals.

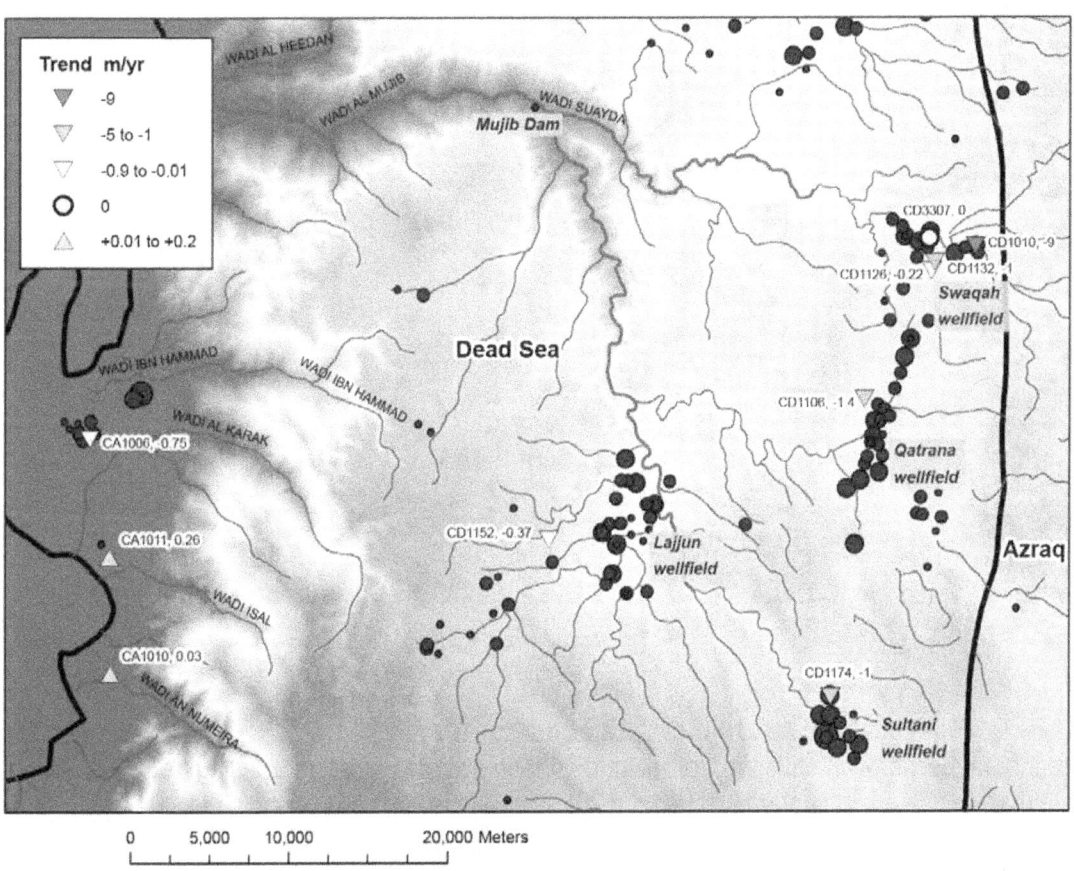

Figure 20. Trends in groundwater levels at selected wells in the central Dead Sea groundwater basin, Jordan. The background colors represent land-surface altitude in meters, ranging from -461 (brown) to 2796 (blue). The groundwater-level trend in 2010, in meters per year, is shown for all wells with data in 2009 or later. Negative trends indicate declining water levels. The dark-blue dots are production wells, and the size of the dot represents the annual withdrawal from each well in 2009. Blue lines are stream channels. (Data provided by Ministry of Water and Irrigation, Jordan; m/yr, meters per year)

The southern part of the Dead Sea groundwater basin includes the stream network of Wadi Al Hasa. Of the 8 groundwater wells with sufficient data in this area, 6 had downward trends, and 2 had flat trends (fig. 21). Groundwater levels were declining most rapidly in the pumping center near the mouth of Wadi Al Hasa. The highest rate of water-level decline was -0.82 m/yr at well CA1082. The rate of groundwater-level decline in the southern part of the Dead Sea basin was less than in the central and northern parts of the basin.

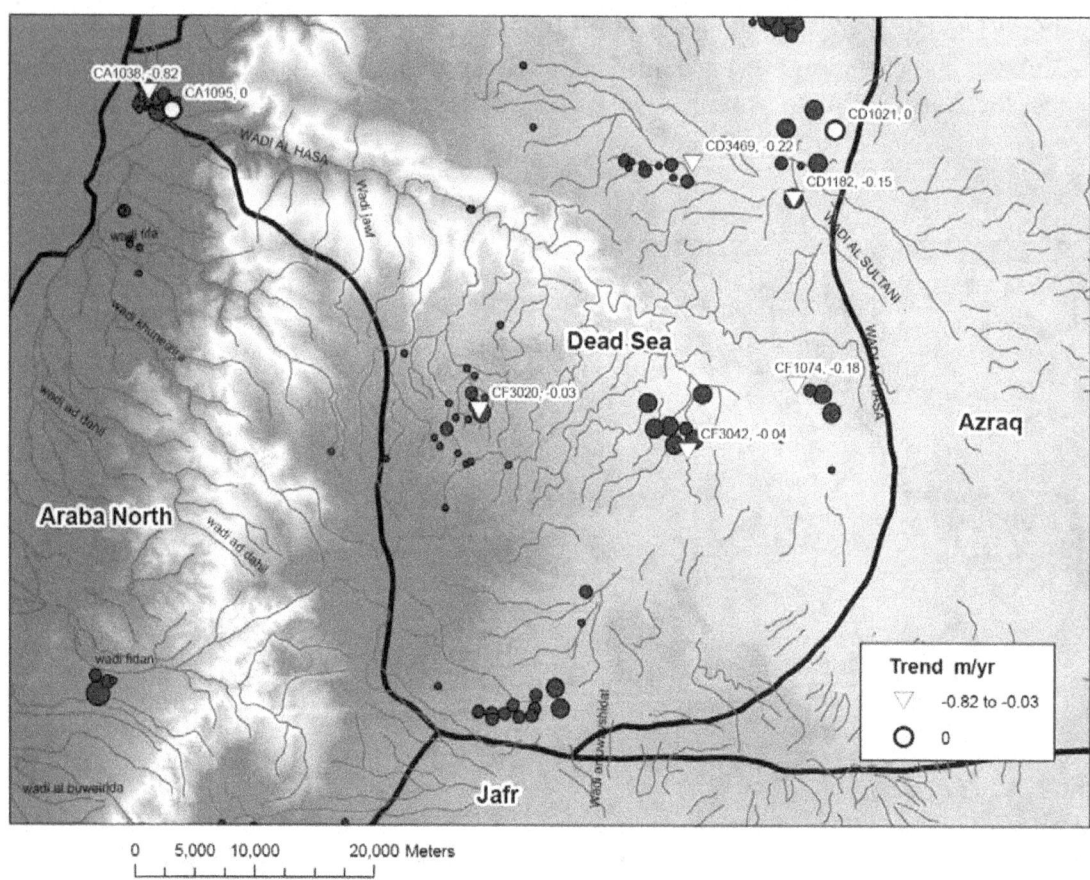

Figure 21.   Trends in groundwater levels at selected wells in the southern Dead Sea groundwater basin, Jordan. The background colors represent land-surface altitude in meters, ranging from -461 (brown) to 2796 (blue). The groundwater-level trend in 2010, in meters per year, is shown for all wells with data in 2009 or later. Negative trends indicate declining water levesl. The dark-blue dots are production wells, and the size of the dot represents the annual withdrawal from each well in 2009. Blue lines are stream channels. (Data provided by Ministry of Water and Irrigation, Jordan; m/yr, meters per year)

Aquifer-thickness and well-depth data were available for 20 wells in the Dead Sea groundwater basin. The water-level trends were used to forecast the saturated thickness in 2030 (table 4; fig. 22), as a percent of the initial saturated thickness or the total saturated thickness. For 2030, the average saturated thickness at the monitoring wells in the Dead Sea basin was forecast to be 61 percent of the initial or total saturated thickness. Three wells were forecast to be dry by 2030 (table 4)

30

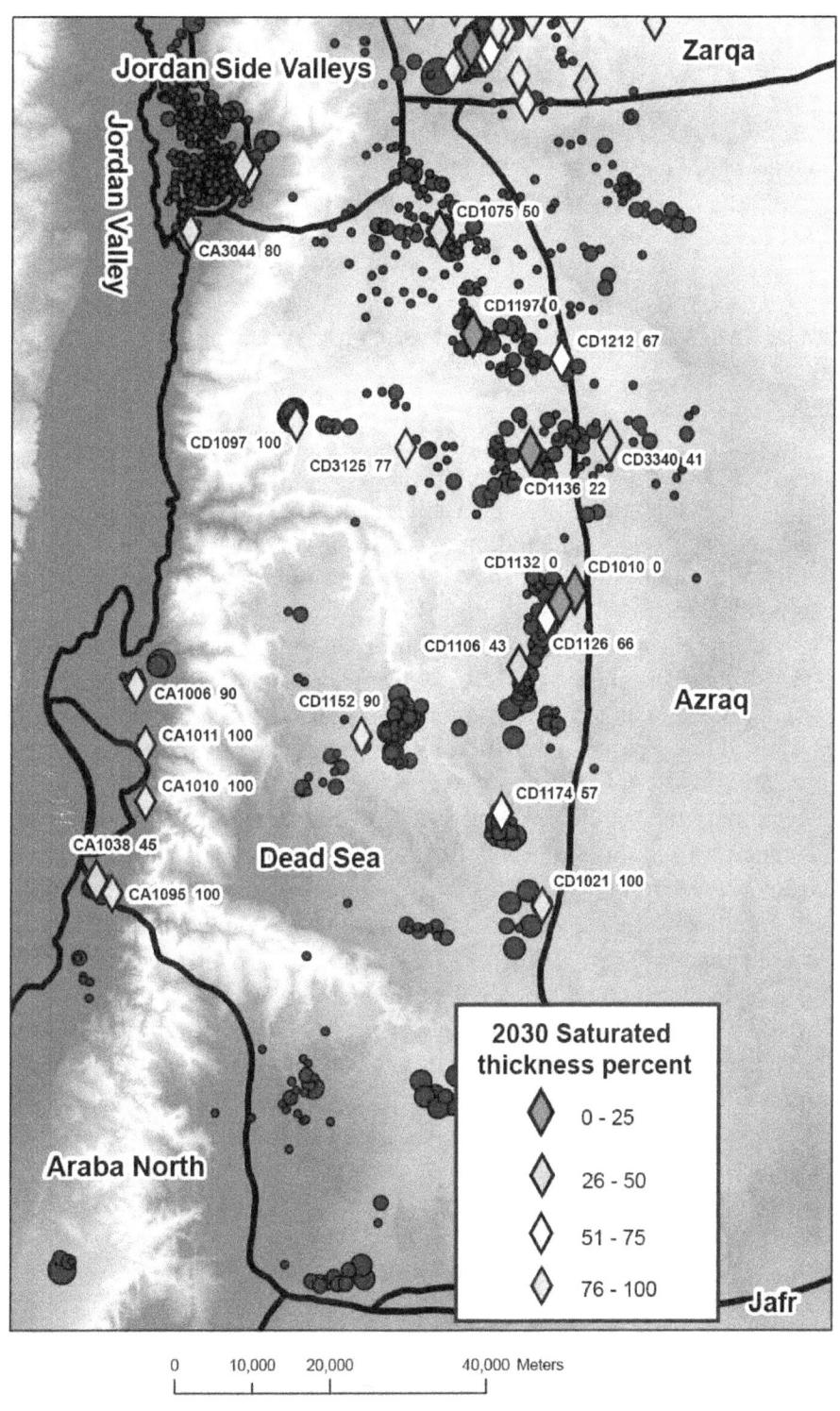

Figure 22. Forecast saturated aquifer thickness in 2030 at selected wells in the Dead Sea groundwater basin, Jordan. The background colors represent land-surface altitude in meters, ranging from lower than 400 (brown) to higher than 900 (blue). The dark-blue dots are production wells, and the size of the dot represents the annual withdrawal from each well in 2009. (Data provided by Ministry of Water and Irrigation, Jordan)

31

Salinity

Groundwater EC trends were variable in the Dead Sea groundwater basin. Twenty-eight wells had adequate data for analysis of EC trends in 2010; EC was increasing at 12 wells, flat (-5 to +5 μS/cm/yr) at 9 wells, and decreasing at 7 wells (table 5).

Table 5. Groundwater electrical-conductivity trends at selected wells in the Dead Sea groundwater basin, Jordan. [*Link*]

The variability in EC was large at many of the wells, and the R^2 ranged from 0.0 to 0.96. The trend estimates are considered highly uncertain because of the variable strength of linear fits to the data, as measured by R^2, and the small number of EC measurements at many locations (table 5). The quality of the fit of the linear trend over time and the scatter of data around this trend line are graphically illustrated in Appendix B for all wells studied.

Increasing and decreasing EC trends were observed throughout the Dead Sea groundwater basin. Of the 9 groundwater wells with sufficient data in the northern part of the Dead Sea groundwater basin, which includes the major intermittent streams Wadi Heedan and Wadi Wala, areas contributing base flow to Wadi Zarqa Ma'een, and springs near the Dead Sea, the EC trend was decreasing at 1 well, flat at 3 wells, and increasing at 5 wells (fig. 23). Six of the wells are clustered near the Wadi Wala dam and downstream well fields. These wells showed contrasting trends ranging from -30.5 to +20.91 μS/cm/yr. Groundwater levels increased after construction of Wadi Wala dam likely as a result of enhanced recharge from the captured flood waters. The remaining three wells are at higher altitudes in areas of distributed pumping, and the EC trend at these wells ranged from +4.27 to +8.95 μS/cm/yr. No wells located in the area of Wadi Zarqa Ma'een had current and adequate data for analysis.

The EC trends were variable in the central part of the Dead Sea groundwater basin, which includes the western part of the surface-water drainage basin for Wadi Mujib. Of the 16 wells with current data, the EC was decreasing at 6 wells, flat at 4 wells, and increasing at 6 wells, ranging from -89 to +59 μS/cm/yr (fig. 24). The two wells with the highest rates of increase are located in a pumping center near the Dead Sea and in the Lajjun well field.

EC data were limited in the southern part of the Dead Sea groundwater basin, which includes the major intermittent stream Wadi Al Hasa. Only three wells had current EC data, and the EC trends were -1.51 (flat), +2.6 (flat), and +285 μS/cm/yr (fig. 25). The highest rate of EC increase was in a pumping center near the Dead Sea.

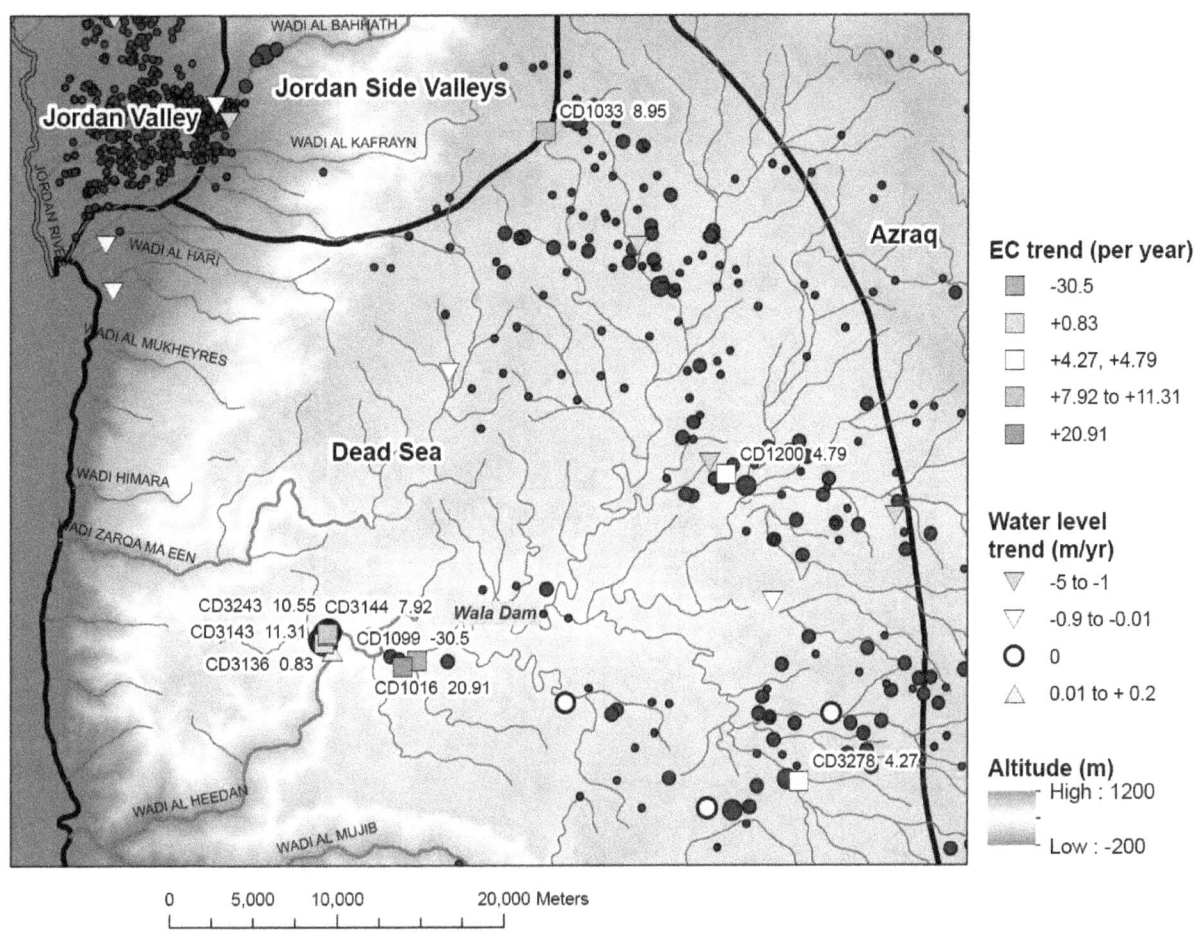

Figure 23. Trends in groundwater electrical conductivity (EC) at selected wells in the northern Dead Sea groundwater basin, Jordan. The background colors represent land-surface altitude in meters. The long-term groundwater EC trend, in microsiemens per centimeter per year, is shown for all wells with data in 2009 or later by colored squares. Triangles and light-green circles represent the current groundwater-level trends (see fig. 19). The dark-blue dots are production wells, and the size of the dot represents the annual withdrawal from each well. Blue lines are stream channels. (Data provided by Ministry of Water and Irrigation, Jordan; m, meters; yr, year)

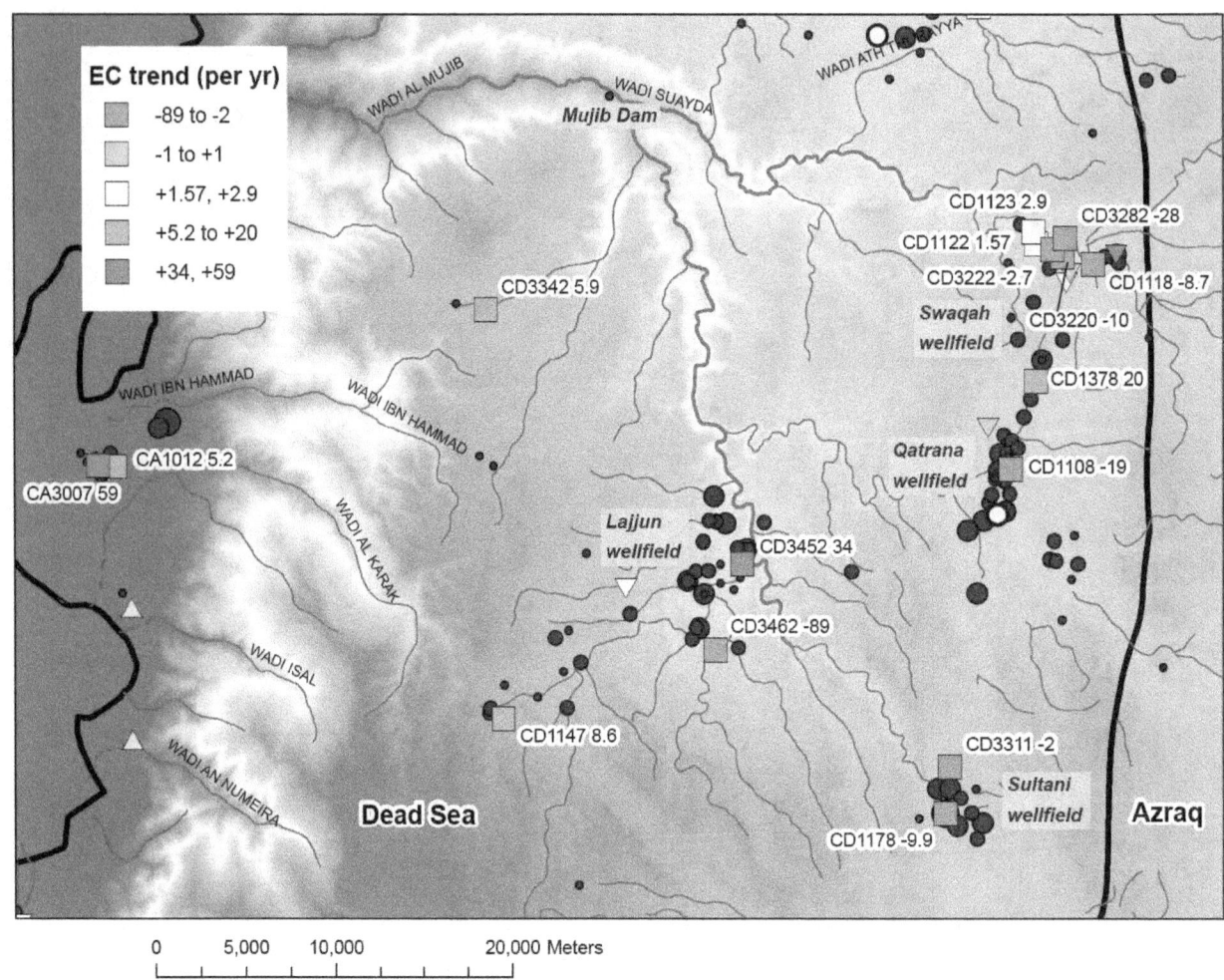

Figure 24. Trends in groundwater electrical-conductivity (EC) at selected wells in the central Dead Sea groundwater basin, Jordan. The background colors represent land-surface altitude in meters, ranging from lower than -200 (brown) to higher than 1200 (blue). The long-term groundwater EC trend, in microsiemens per centimeter per year, is shown for all wells with data in 2009 or later by colored squares. Triangles and light-green circles represent the current groundwater-level trends (see fig. 20). The dark-blue dots are production wells, and the size of the dot represents the annual withdrawal from each well. Blue lines are stream channels. (Data provided by Ministry of Water and Irrigation, Jordan; yr, year)

34

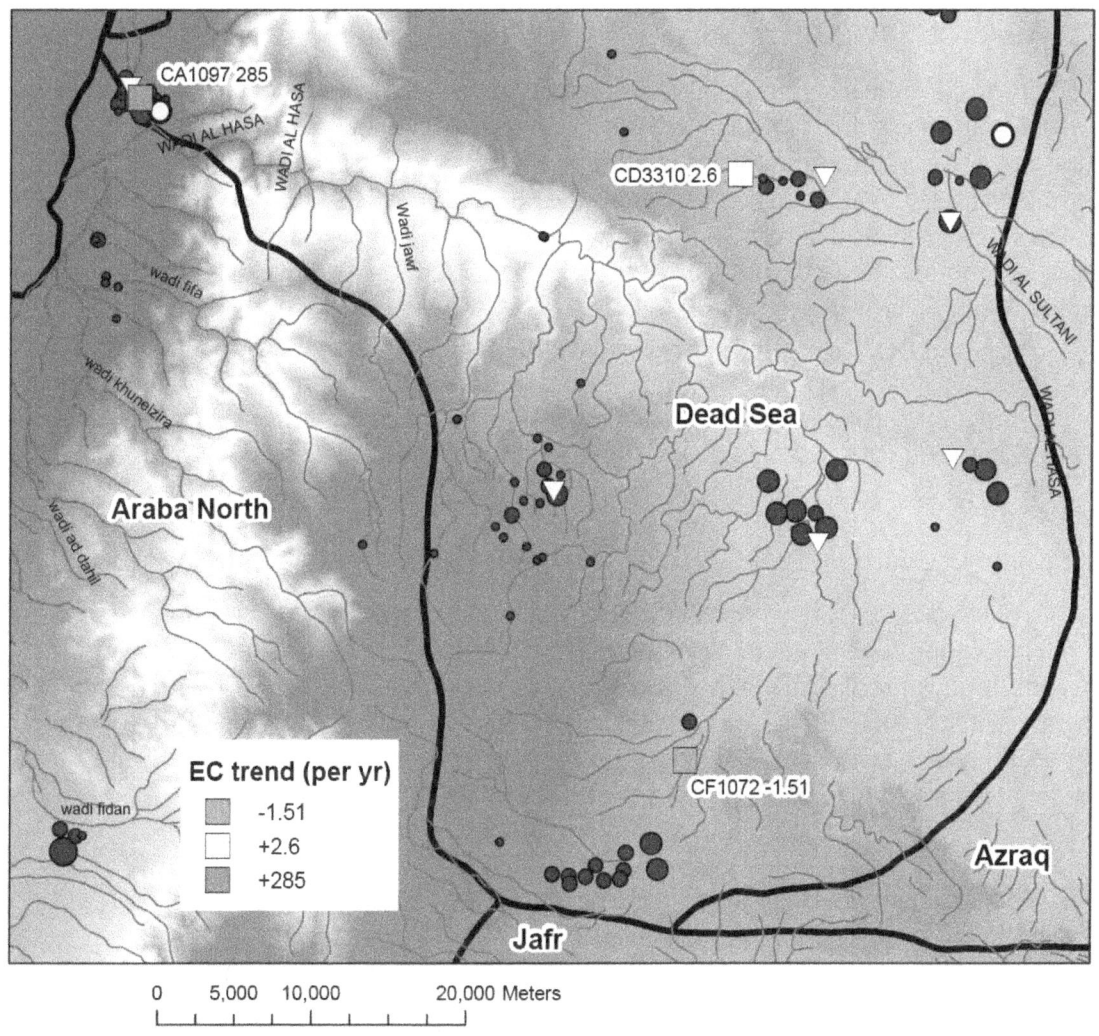

Figure 25. Trends in groundwater electrical-conductivity (EC) at selected wells in the southern Dead Sea groundwater basin, Jordan. The background colors represent land-surface altitude in meters, ranging from lower than -200 (brown) to higher than 1200 (blue). The long-term groundwater EC trend, in microsiemens per centimeter per year, is shown for all wells with data in 2009 or later by colored squares. Triangles and light-green circles represent the current groundwater-level trends (see fig. 22). The dark-blue dots are production wells, and the size of the dot represents the annual withdrawal from each well. Blue lines are stream channels. (Data provided by Ministry of Water and Irrigation, Jordan, yr, year)

Hammad Groundwater Basin

The arid Hammad groundwater basin is located in the northeastern part of Jordan and experiences much less recharge than the western basins (Salameh and Bannayan, 1993). In addition to local flood recharge in the winter, groundwater flow enters the basin in Jordan from the north, where recharge occurs at higher altitudes. The basin has been studied by many authors, including Bajjali and Abu-Jaber (2001), who report ages of groundwater exceeding 10,000 years for samples from Hammad basin wells. Generally, long residence times of groundwater are associated with high salinity.

There are few monitoring wells, and few wells of any type, in the Hammad basin. No monitoring wells are close to the largest pumping center in the Hammad basin. Neither of the two wells previously studied (David W. Clark, USGS, written commun., 2002) had current (2009 or later) water-level data in the database. One of those wells was identified as a production well in the WIS database.

Groundwater Levels

Groundwater levels in available monitoring wells in the Hammad groundwater basin did not have large long-term changes according to the current analysis of data from 1971 to 2010. Four monitoring wells had adequate data for analysis of water-level trends in 2010; trends were downward at two wells, flat at one well, and upward at one well (table 6; fig. 26). The maximum rate of groundwater-level decline was -0.21 m/yr, and the trend was +0.19 m/yr at the single well with rising levels. All groundwater-level trend graphs are provided in Appendix C.

Table 6. Groundwater-level trends and forecast saturated aquifer thicknesses at selected wells in the Hammad groundwater basin, Jordan. [*Link*]

Where aquifer-thickness and well-depth data were available, the groundwater-level trends were used to forecast the aquifer saturated thickness in 2030 (table 6; fig. 27), as a percent of the initial saturated thickness or the total aquifer saturated thickness. For 2030, the average saturated thickness at the monitoring wells in the Hammad basin was forecast to be 98 percent of the initial or total aquifer saturated thickness.

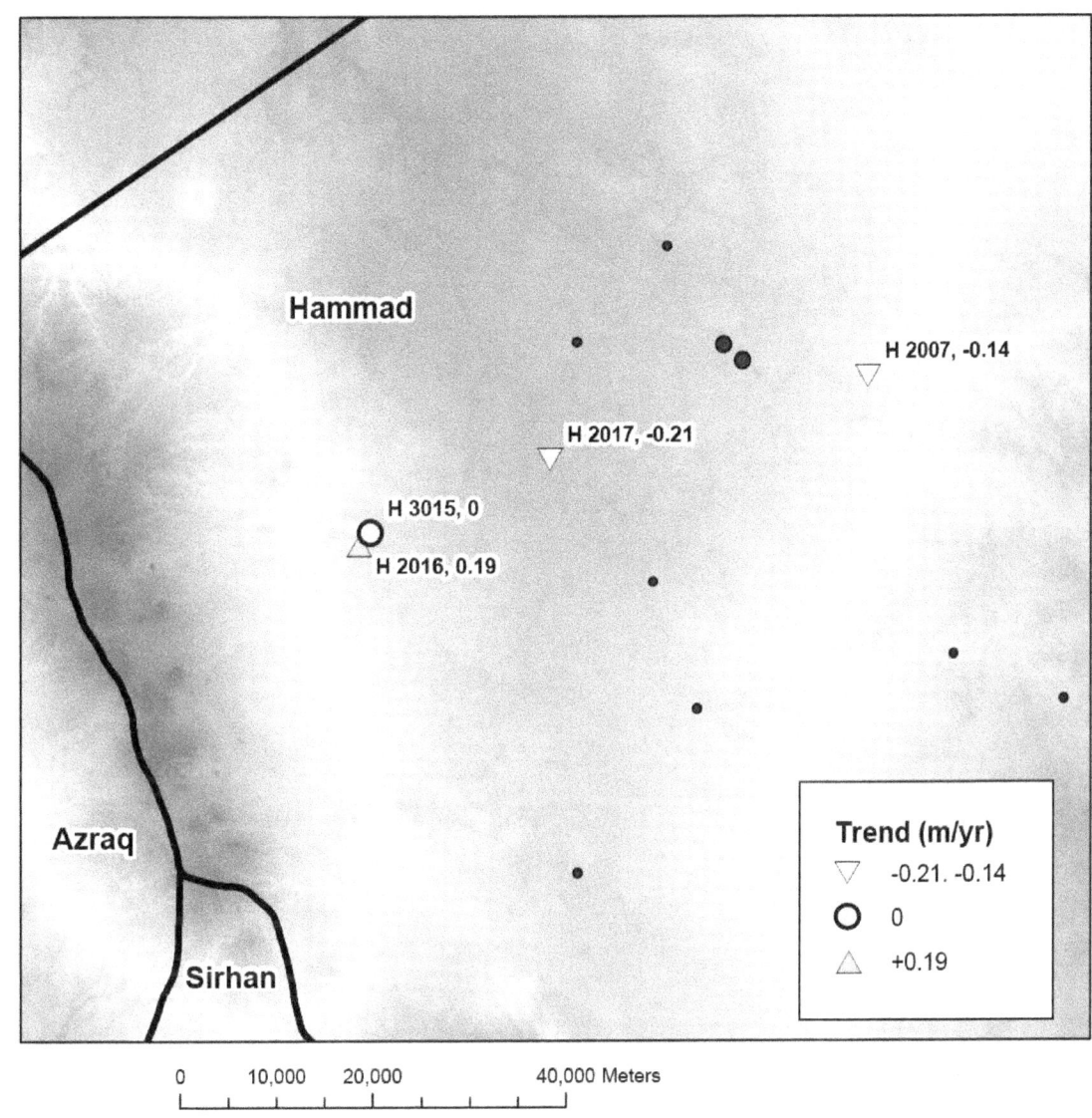

Figure 26.   Trends in groundwater levels at selected wells in the Hammad groundwater basin, Jordan. The background colors represent land-surface altitude in meters, ranging from lower than 550 (brown) to higher than 950 (blue). The groundwater-level trend in 2010, in meters per year, is shown for all monitoring wells with data in 2009 or later. Negative trends indicate declining water levels. The dark-blue dots are production wells, and the size of the dot represents the annual withdrawal from each well in 2009. (Data provided by Ministry of Water and Irrigation, Jordan; m/yr, meters per year)

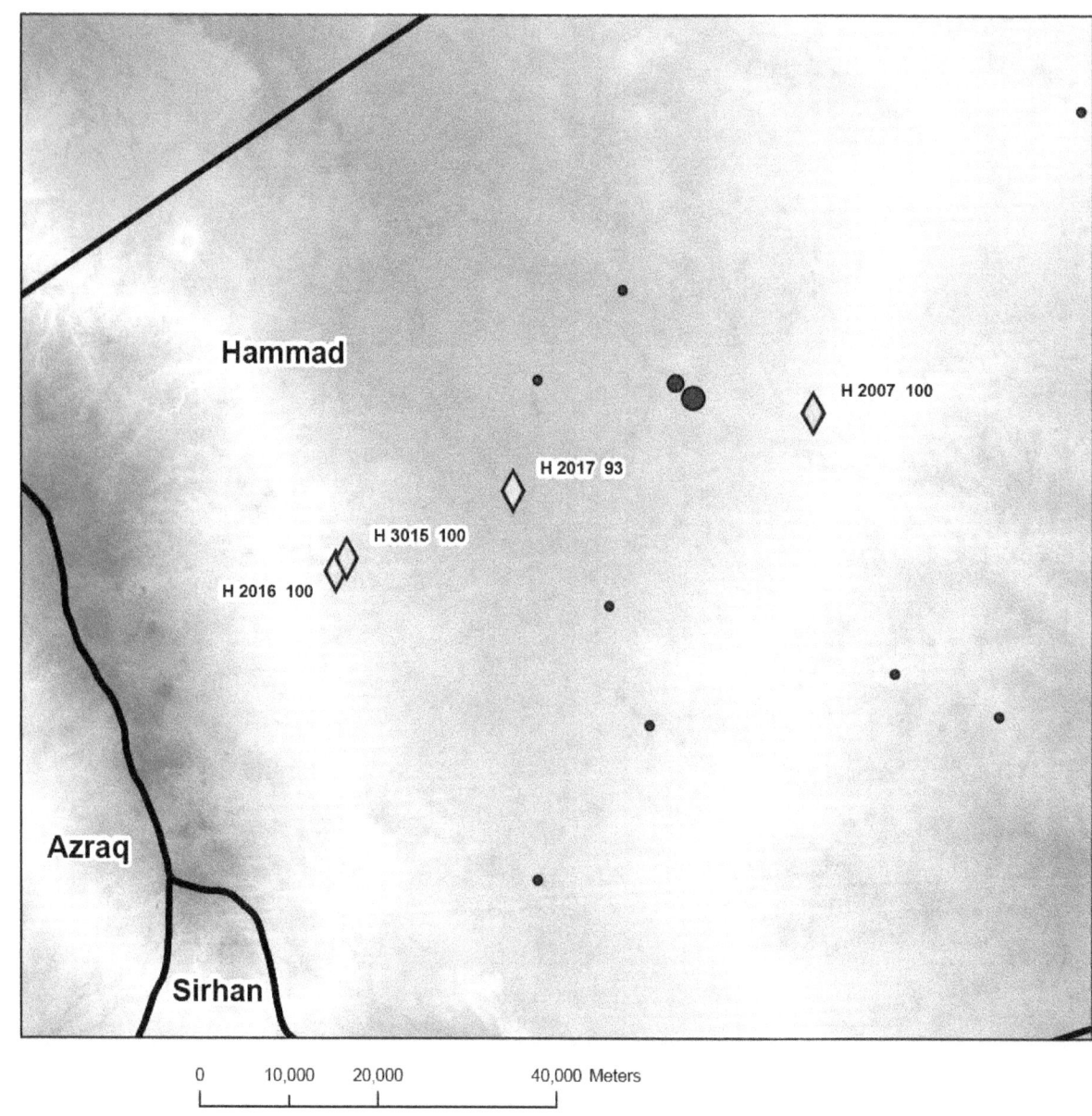

Figure 27. Forecast saturated aquifer thickness in 2030, in percent, at selected wells in the Hammad groundwater basin, Jordan. The green diamonds are wells where saturated thickness was forecast, and the adjacent numbers are the well identifier and the saturated thickness value. The background colors represent land-surface altitude in meters, ranging from lower than 550 (brown) to higher than 950 (blue). The dark-blue dots are production wells, and the size of the dot represents the annual withdrawal from each well in 2009. (Data provided by Ministry of Water and Irrigation, Jordan)

Salinity

Groundwater trends in salinity, as indicated by trends in EC, were variable in the Hammad groundwater basin, although there were relatively few wells. Only four wells in the database had current (2009 or later) data. The criterion for selecting wells with current data was changed to 2006 or later, in order that two more wells could be used for the trend analysis. Of these six wells, groundwater EC trends were upward at four wells, flat (-5 to +5 µS/cm/yr) at one well, and downward at one well (table 7). Additional wells could have been analyzed for current trends if additional data in 2006 or later had been available.

Table 7. Groundwater electrical-conductivity trends at selected wells in the Hammad groundwater basin, Jordan. [*Link*]

Groundwater EC trends were variable in the Hammad groundwater basin (fig. 28). The variability in EC was large at many wells, and the linear trend regression R^2 ranged from 0.02 to 0.77. In general, the trend estimates are considered highly uncertain because of the variable strength of linear fits to the data as measured by R^2 and the small number of EC measurements at many locations (table 7). The quality of the fit of the linear trend over time and the scatter of data around this trend line are graphically illustrated in Appendix C for all wells studied.

Although groundwater levels were not declining rapidly in the Hammad basin, most of the wells showed moderate rates of EC increase, and all the wells had higher EC than was generally found in the other basins. This is likely due to the low recharge in this arid basin and the long residence time of groundwater. The six wells studied are clustered in two locations within the basin. Local variability was illustrated by the single well in the Rwaished area (H 3060) that showed EC decreasing, in contrast to three nearby wells with increasing EC.

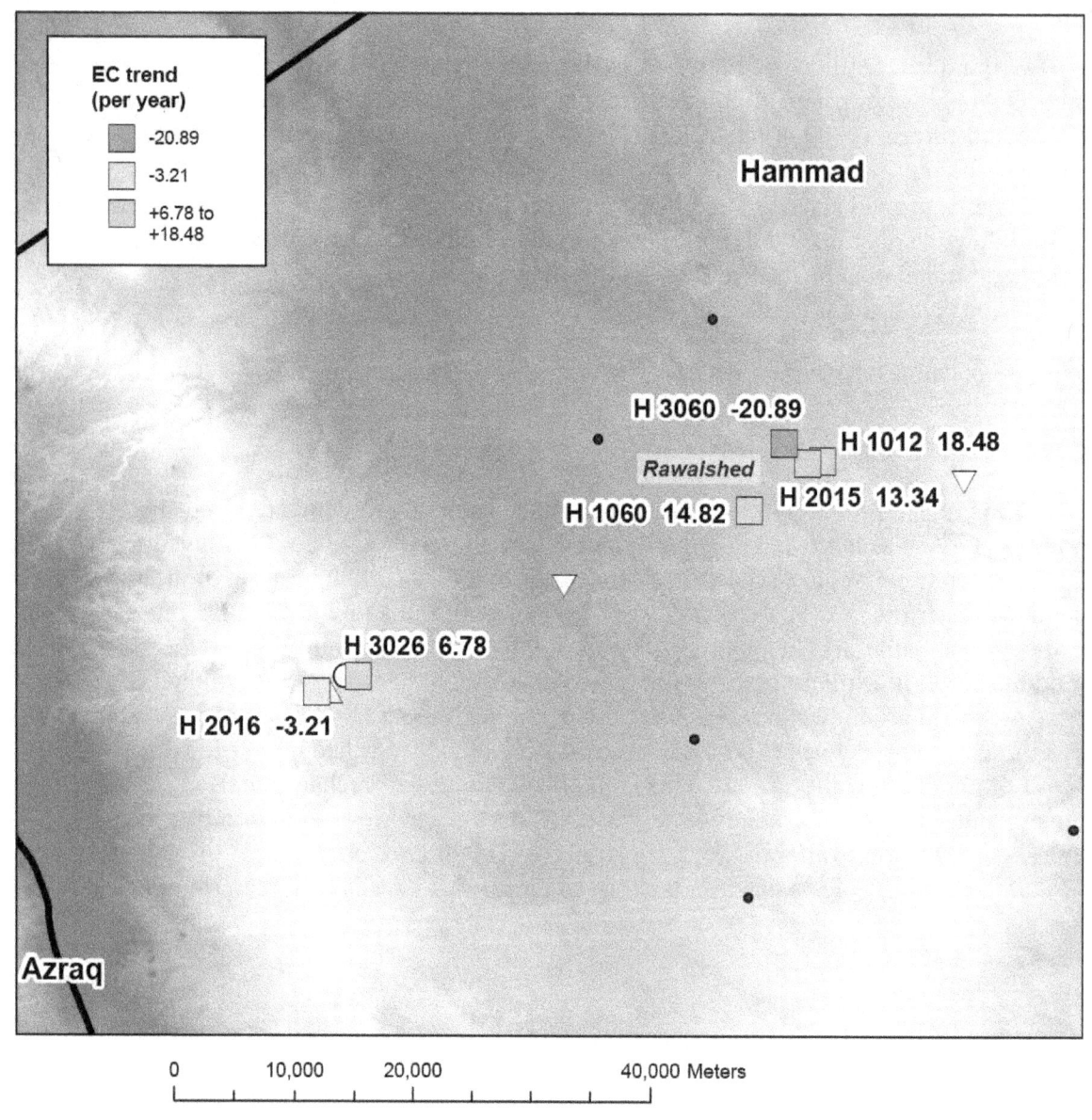

Figure 28. Trends in electrical conductivity (EC) at selected wells in the Hammad groundwater basin, Jordan. The background colors represent land-surface altitude in meters, ranging from lower than 600 (brown) to higher than 900 (blue). The long-term groundwater EC trend, in microsiemens per centimeter per year, is shown for all monitoring wells with adequate data in 2006 or later by colored squares. Negative trends indicate decreasing EC. Triangles and light-green circles represent the current groundwater-level trend (see fig. 26). The dark-blue dots are production wells, and the size of the dot represents the annual withdrawal from each well in 2009. (Data provided by Ministry of Water and Irrigation, Jordan)

Jordan Side Valleys Groundwater Basin

The Jordan Side Valleys groundwater basin (see Figure 1) receives most recharge in the highlands in the eastern part of the basin, and groundwater flow is generally from east to west, towards the Jordan Valley (Salameh and Bannayan, 1993). Numerous springs occur at mid and lower altitudes. Background information on the groundwater resources of the Wadi Al Arab well field area in the northern part of the Jordan Side Valleys basin is presented by Subah and others (2006).

Groundwater Levels

Groundwater levels were declining in the Jordan Side Valleys groundwater basin (figs. 29, 30). Nine of 11 monitoring wells had adequate data for analysis of water-level trends in 2010. Of these, groundwater levels were declining at seven wells and were flat at two wells (table 8). The maximum rate of groundwater-level decline was -9 m/yr near a pumping center along the Zarqa River (fig. 30). Groundwater levels were previously studied for two monitoring wells in the basin (David W. Clark, USGS, written commun., 2002); these two and an additional seven wells had current monitoring data in the database. However, monitoring wells were not available in several areas of pumping in the Jordan Side Valleys groundwater basin, particularly in the northern part of the basin (fig. 29). Pumping from wells occurred primarily along the western edge of the basin, near the Jordan Valley, in the highlands on the eastern edge of the basin, and along wadis. Few wells are present in the basin interior.

Table 8. Groundwater-level trends and forecast saturated aquifer thicknesses at selected wells in the Jordan Side Valleys groundwater basin, Jordan. [*Link*]

For 2030, the average saturated thickness at the 9 monitoring wells in the Jordan Side Valleys basin was forecast to be 64 percent of the initial or total aquifer saturated thickness. The minimum saturated thickness was forecast to be 20 percent (table 8; fig. 31) .

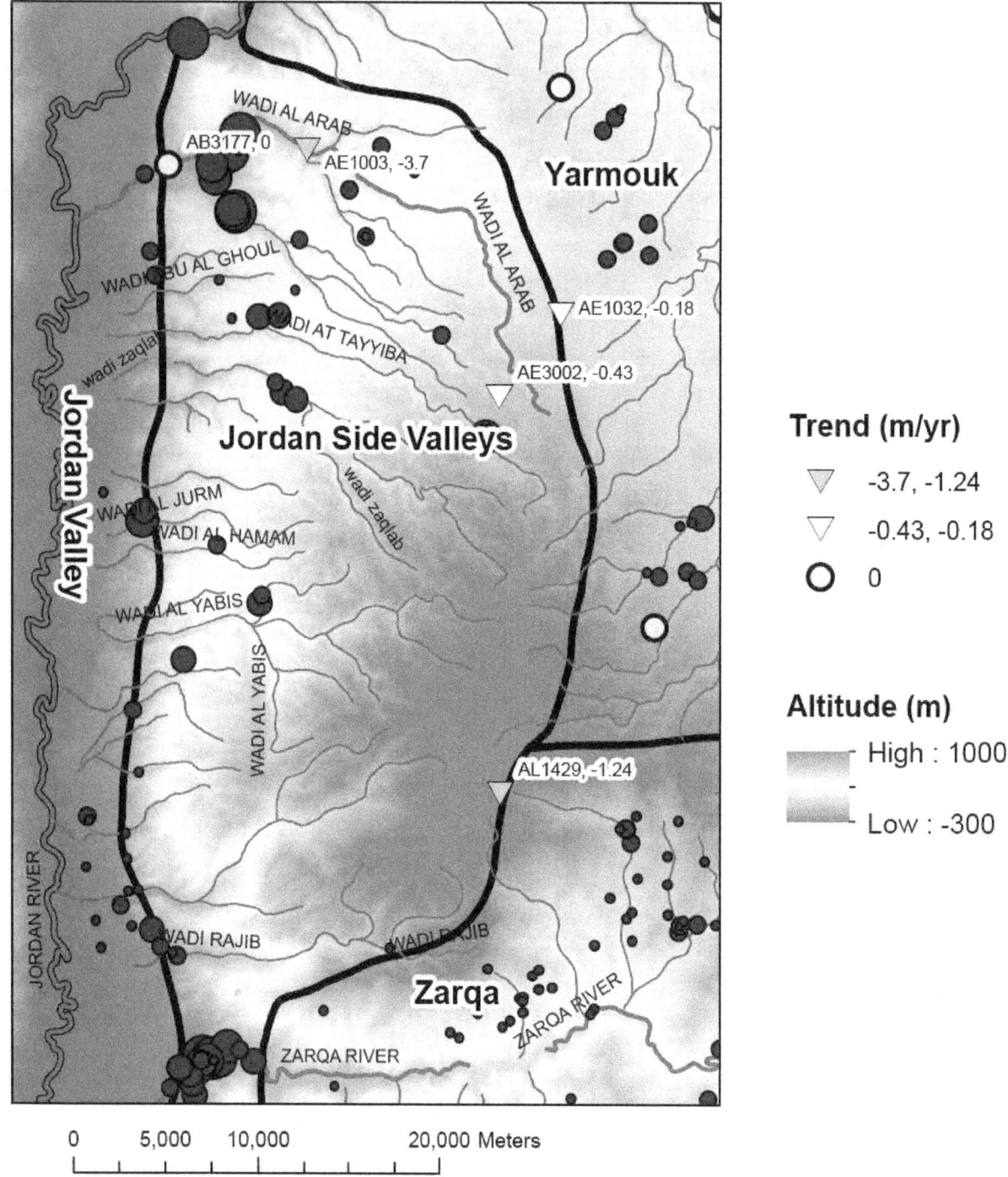

Figure 29.   Trends in groundwater levels at selected wells in the northern part of the Jordan Side Valleys groundwater basin, Jordan. The background colors represent land-surface altitude in meters. The groundwater-level trend in 2010, in meters per year, is shown for all wells with data in 2009 or later. Negative trends indicate declining water levels. The dark-blue dots are production wells, and the size of the dot represents the annual withdrawal from each well in 2009. Blue lines are stream channels. (Data provided by Ministry of Water and Irrigation, Jordan, m, meters; yr, year)

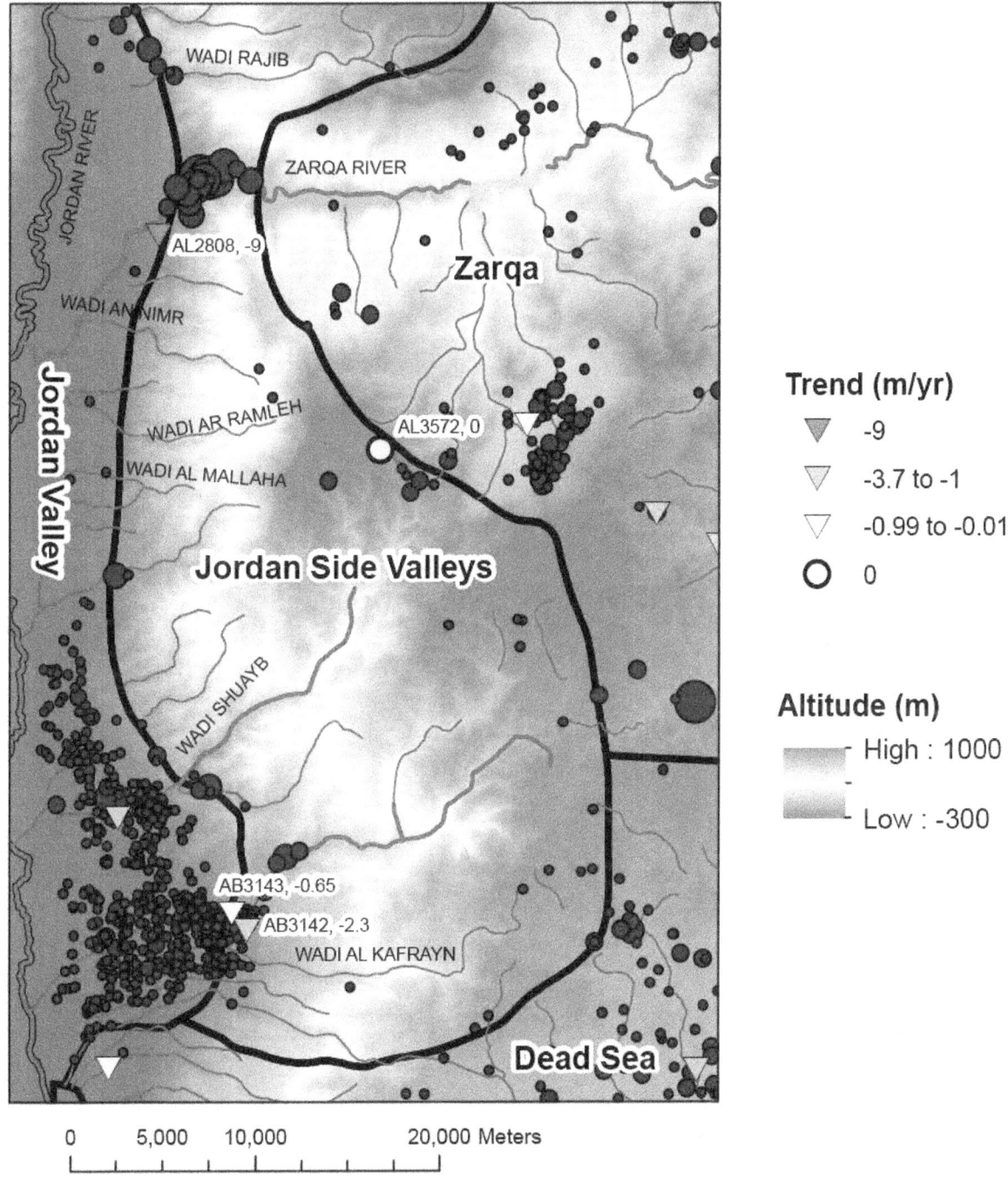

Figure 30. Trends in groundwater levels at selected wells in the southern part of the Jordan Side Valleys groundwater basin, Jordan. The background colors represents land-surface altitude in meters. The groundwater-level trend in 2010, in meters per year, is shown for all wells with data in 2009 or later. Negative trends indicate declining water levels. The dark-blue dots are production wells, and the size of the dot represents the annual withdrawal from each well in 2009. Blue lines are stream channels. (Data provided by Ministry of Water and Irrigation, Jordan; m, meters; yr, year)

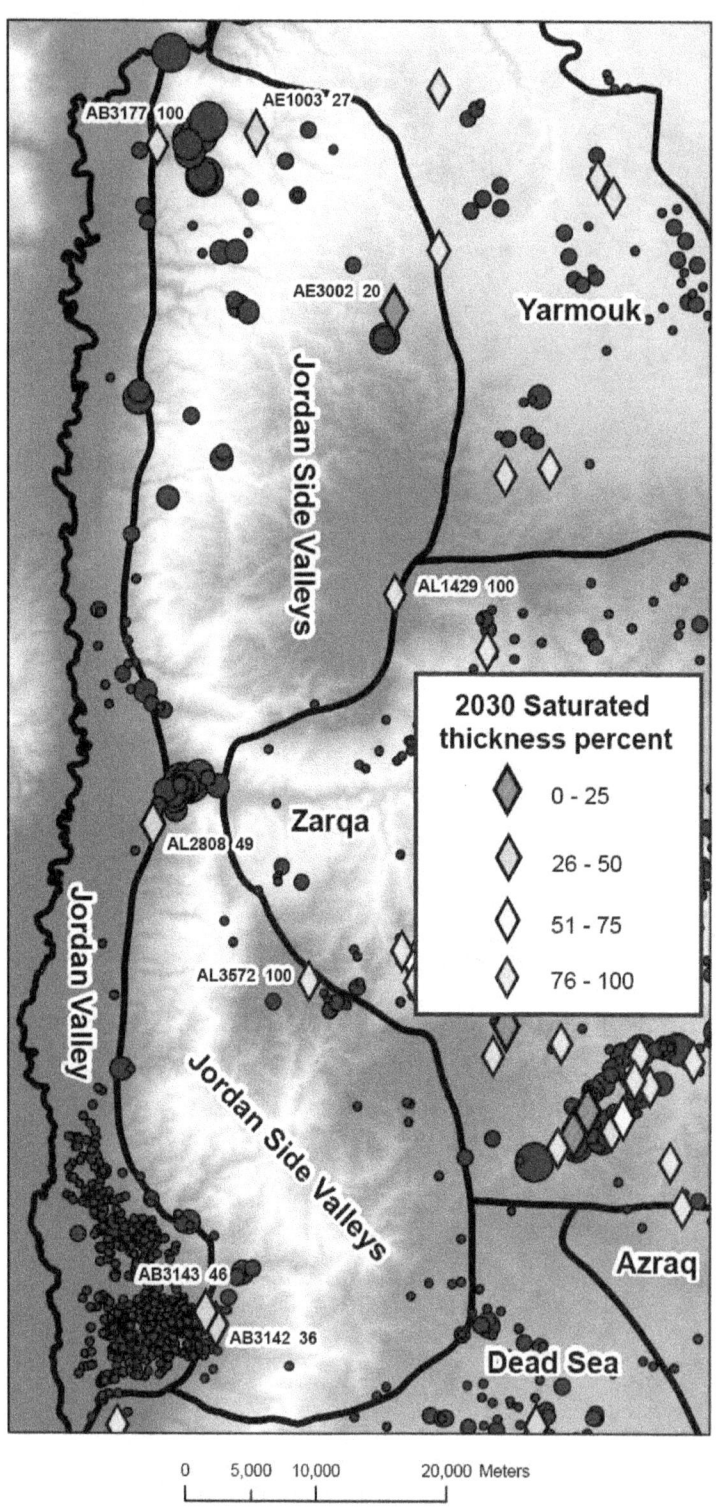

Figure 31. Forecast saturated aquifer thickness in 2030 at selected wells in the Jordan Side Valleys groundwater basin, Jordan. The background colors represent land-surface altitude in meters, ranging from lower than -300 to higher than 1000. The dark-blue dots are production wells, and the size of the dot represents the annual withdrawal from each well in 2009. (Data provided by Ministry of Water and Irrigation, Jordan)

Salinity

Groundwater EC trends were variable in the Jordan Side Valleys groundwater basin. Only 19 wells in the database had current (2009 or later) data. The criterion for selecting wells with current data was changed to 2006 or later, in order that three more wells could be used for the trend analysis. Of these 22 wells, groundwater EC trends were increasing EC at 3 wells, flat (-5 to +5 µS/cm/yr) at 15 wells, and decreasing at 4 wells (table 9). Table 9 and Appendix D include three wells with last measurements made in 1993, 2004, and 2005, but these wells were not used in the statistics or maps in this report.

Table 9. Groundwater electrical-conductivity trends at selected wells in the Jordan Side Valleys groundwater basin, Jordan. [*Link*]

The variability in EC was large at many wells, and the linear trend regression R^2 ranged from 0.0 to 0.91. In general, the trend estimates are considered highly uncertain because of the variable strength of linear fits to the data as measured by R^2 and the small number of EC measurements at many locations (table 9). The quality of the fit of the linear trend over time and the scatter of data around this trend line are graphically illustrated for several examples below. Graphs for all wells studied are in Appendix D.

In the northern part of the Jordan Side Valleys groundwater basin (fig. 32), only one well had an increasing EC trend (well AK1013), and EC trends in the other wells were flat or decreasing. The well with increasing EC trend is at the bottom of the basin near the Jordan Valley. This location near the Jordan River may be affected by deep groundwater rising up to discharge.

The monitoring wells in the southern part of the Jordan Side Valleys groundwater basin showed highly variable EC trends. The EC trends were increasing at two wells, flat at one well, and decreasing at two wells (fig. 33). The well with flat trend is the only well located in the higher altitude of the basin. Both of the wells with increasing EC are located at the western border of the basin near the Jordan Valley and near the ultimate groundwater-discharge locations, the Jordan River and the Dead Sea, where deep groundwater rises to discharge.

45

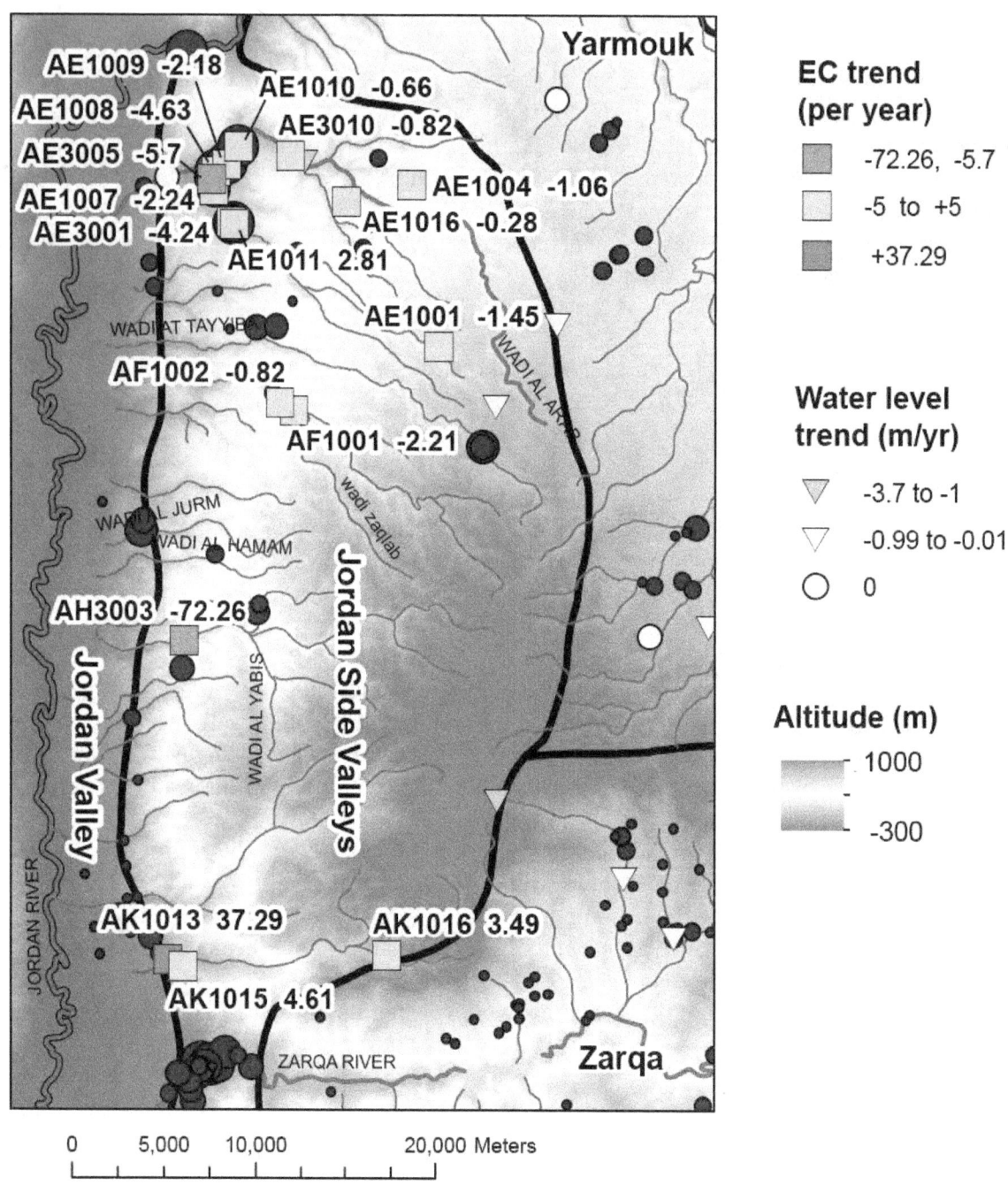

Figure 32. Trends in groundwater electrical conductivity (EC) at selected wells in the northern part of the Jordan Side Valleys groundwater basin, Jordan. The background colors represent land-surface altitude in meters. The long-term groundwater EC trend, in microsiemens per centimeter per year, is shown for all wells with data in 2006 or later. Negative trends indicate decreasing EC. The dark-blue dots are production wells, and the size of the dot represents the annual withdrawal from each well in 2009. Blue lines are stream channels. (Data provided by Ministry of Water and Irrigation, Jordan; m, meters; yr, year)

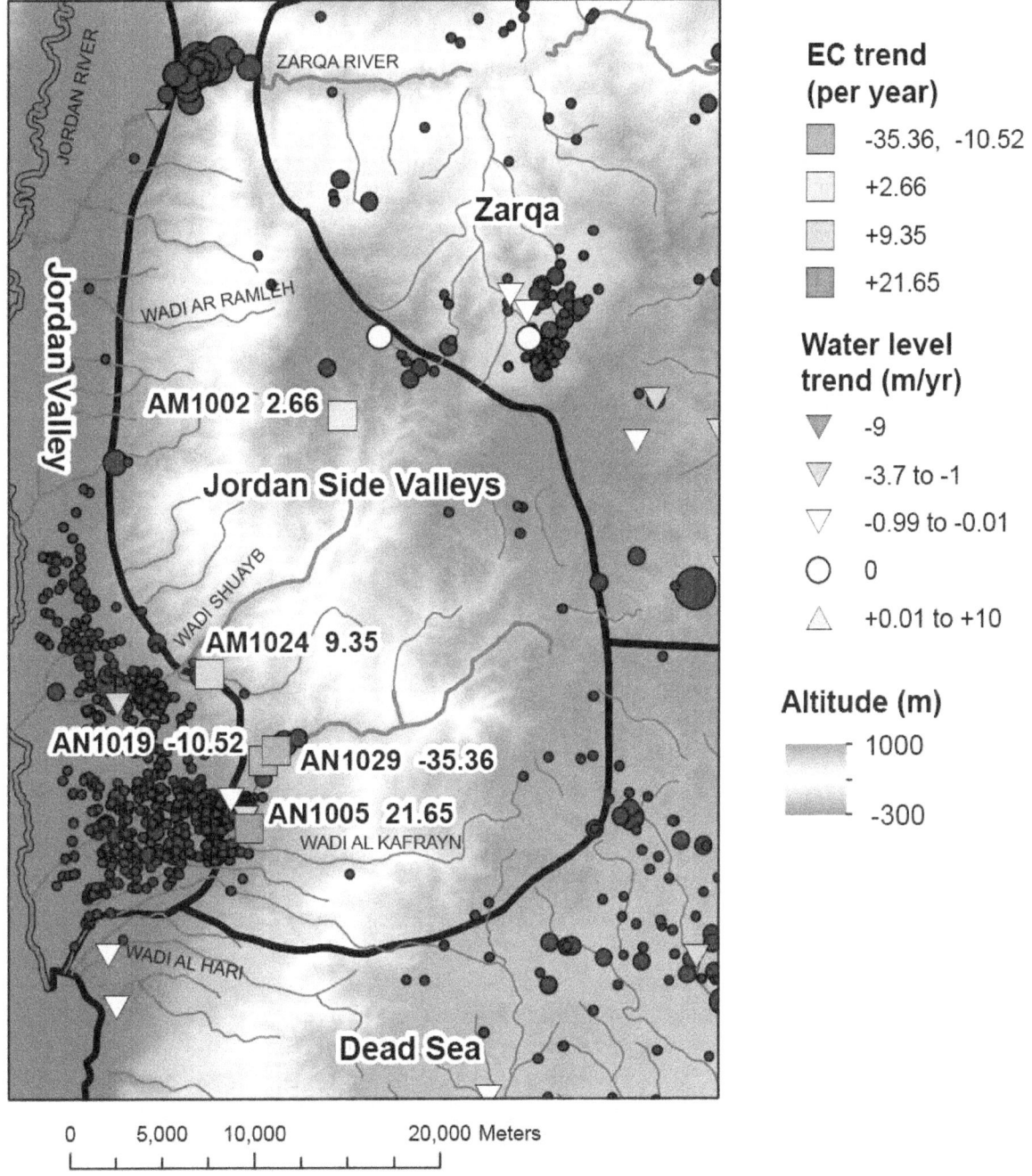

Figure 33. Trends in groundwater electrical conductivity (EC) at selected wells in the southern part of the Jordan Side Valleys groundwater basin, Jordan. The background colors represent land-surface altitude in meters. The groundwater EC trend, in microsiemens per centimeter per year, is shown for all monitoring wells with data in 2006 or later. Negative trends indicate decreasing EC. The dark-blue dots are production wells, and the size of the dot represents the annual withdrawal from each well in 2009. Blue lines are stream channels. (Data provided by Ministry of Water and Irrigation, Jordan; m, meters; yr, year)

Yarmouk Groundwater Basin

The Yarmouk groundwater basin is located in the north of Jordan (fig. 1) where it is recharged by winter precipitation; groundwater inflow is from highlands in the north and west. Groundwater withdrawals are large in the basin. Salameh (2004) describes the Yarmouk basin hydrogeology and water resources, and relates salinity differences and isotopic data. Salinity in the Yarmouk groundwater basin has been studied by numerous authors. Abu-Jaber and Kharabsheh (2008) map salinity in part of the basin and note higher salinities in lower altitude parts of the area. Bajjali (2008) identifies higher salinity associated with a deep aquifer in the basin. Batayneh and others (2008) determine that the salinity and major ion concentrations reflect predominantly rock-dissolution processes.

Groundwater Levels

Groundwater levels were declining in the Yarmouk groundwater basin, especially near pumping centers in the eastern part of the basin in Jordan. Eleven of 13 monitoring wells had adequate data for analysis of groundwater-level trends in 2010. Of these, water-level trends were downward at seven wells, flat at three wells, and upward at one well (table 10; fig. 34). The maximum rate of groundwater-level decline was -3.7 m/yr, and the rate of groundwater-level rise was +0.25 m/yr at the single well with rising levels. All groundwater-level trend graphs are provided in Appendix E.

Table 10. Groundwater-level trends and forecast saturated aquifer thicknesses at selected wells in the Yarmouk groundwater basin, Jordan. [*Link*]

Monitoring wells were not available for several areas of pumping in the Yarmouk basin. In particular, groundwater levels near pumping centers in the central part of the Yarmouk basin (fig. 34) are not represented by the monitoring well network.

Where aquifer-thickness and well-depth data were available, the groundwater-level trends were used to forecast the saturated thickness in 2030 (table 10; fig. 35) as a percent of the initial saturated thickness or the total saturated thickness. For 2030, the average saturated thickness at the monitoring wells in the Yarmouk basin was forecast to be 66 percent of the initial or total saturated thickness. Of the 11 wells with adequate aquifer-thickness and well-depth data, one well was forecast to be dry by 2030, and one well was forecast to be saturated over only 16 percent of the total aquifer thickness.

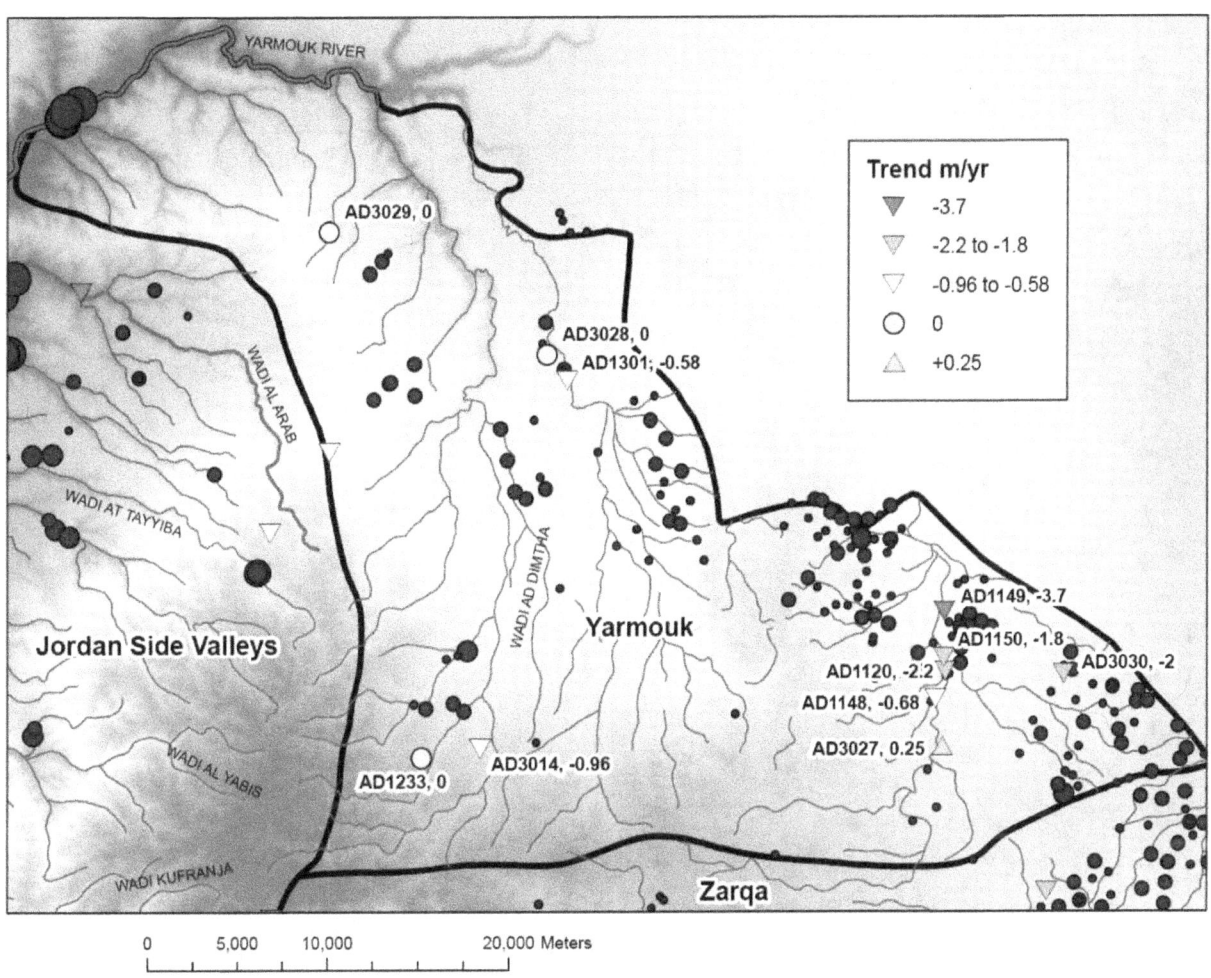

Figure 34. Trends in groundwater levels at selected wells in the Yarmouk groundwater basin, Jordan. The background colors represent land-surface altitude in meters, ranging from lower than 0 (brown) to higher than 1100 (blue). The groundwater-level trend in 2010, in meters per year, is shown for all wells with data in 2009 or later. Negative trends indicate declining water levels. The dark-blue dots are production wells, and the size of the dot represents the annual withdrawal from each well in 2009. Blue lines are stream channels. (Data provided by Ministry of Water and Irrigation, Jordan; m/yr, meters per year)

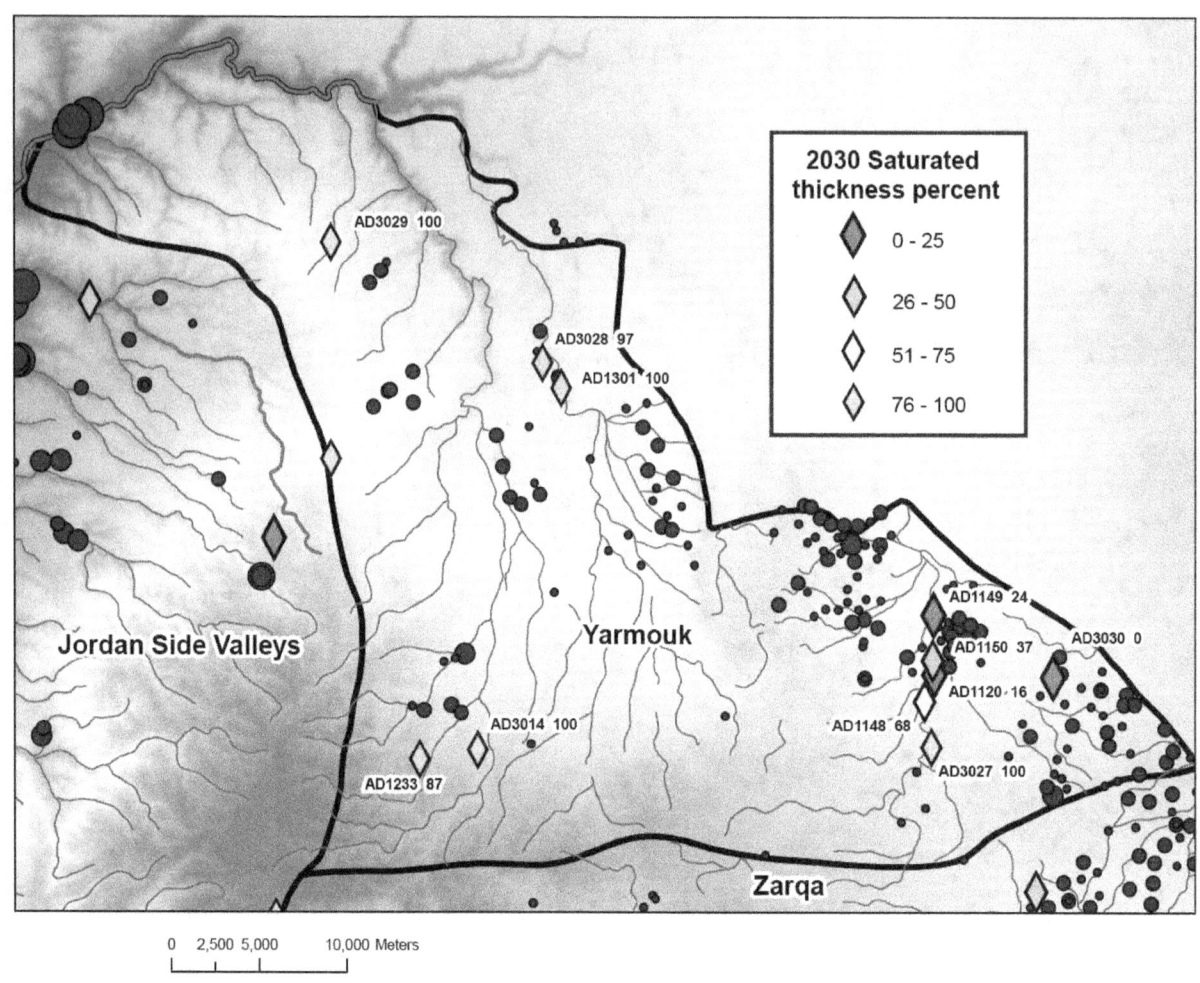

Figure 35. Forecast saturated aquifer thickness in 2030, at selected wells in the Yarmouk groundwater basin, Jordan. The background colors represent land-surface altitude in meters, ranging from lower than 0 (brown) to higher than 1100 (blue). The dark-blue dots are production wells, and the size of the dot represents the annual withdrawal from each well. Blue lines are stream channels. (Data provided by Ministry of Water and Irrigation, Jordan)

Salinity

Groundwater EC trends were variable in the Yarmouk groundwater basin. Sixteen wells in the database have current (2009 or later) data. Of these 16 wells, groundwater EC trends were increasing at 3 wells, flat (-5 to +5 μS/cm/yr) at 10 wells, and decreasing at 3 wells (table 11).

Table 11. Groundwater electrical-conductivity trends at selected wells in the Yarmouk groundwater basin, Jordan. [*Link*]

The EC trends varied greatly for all wells, and the linear trend regression R^2 ranged from 0.0 to 0.95 (table 11). In general, the trend estimates are considered highly uncertain because of the variable strength of linear fits to the data, as measured by R^2, and the small number of EC measurements at many locations (table 11). The quality of the fit of the linear trend over time and the scatter of data around this trend line are graphically illustrated for all wells studied in Appendix E.

Groundwater EC trends varied spatially in the Yarmouk groundwater basin (fig. 36). The trends were relatively flat in the western highlands. Substantially increasing EC occurred at a deep well (AD1295); shallower wells in this area also showed increasing EC. However, most wells showed flat EC over time. Several wells in the southeastern part of the basin had decreasing EC. The variability of trends, and current EC values, are likely related to local hydrogeologic and flow conditions. Several areas, including major pumping areas along the Yarmouk River, did not have adequate EC data for an evaluation of current trends.

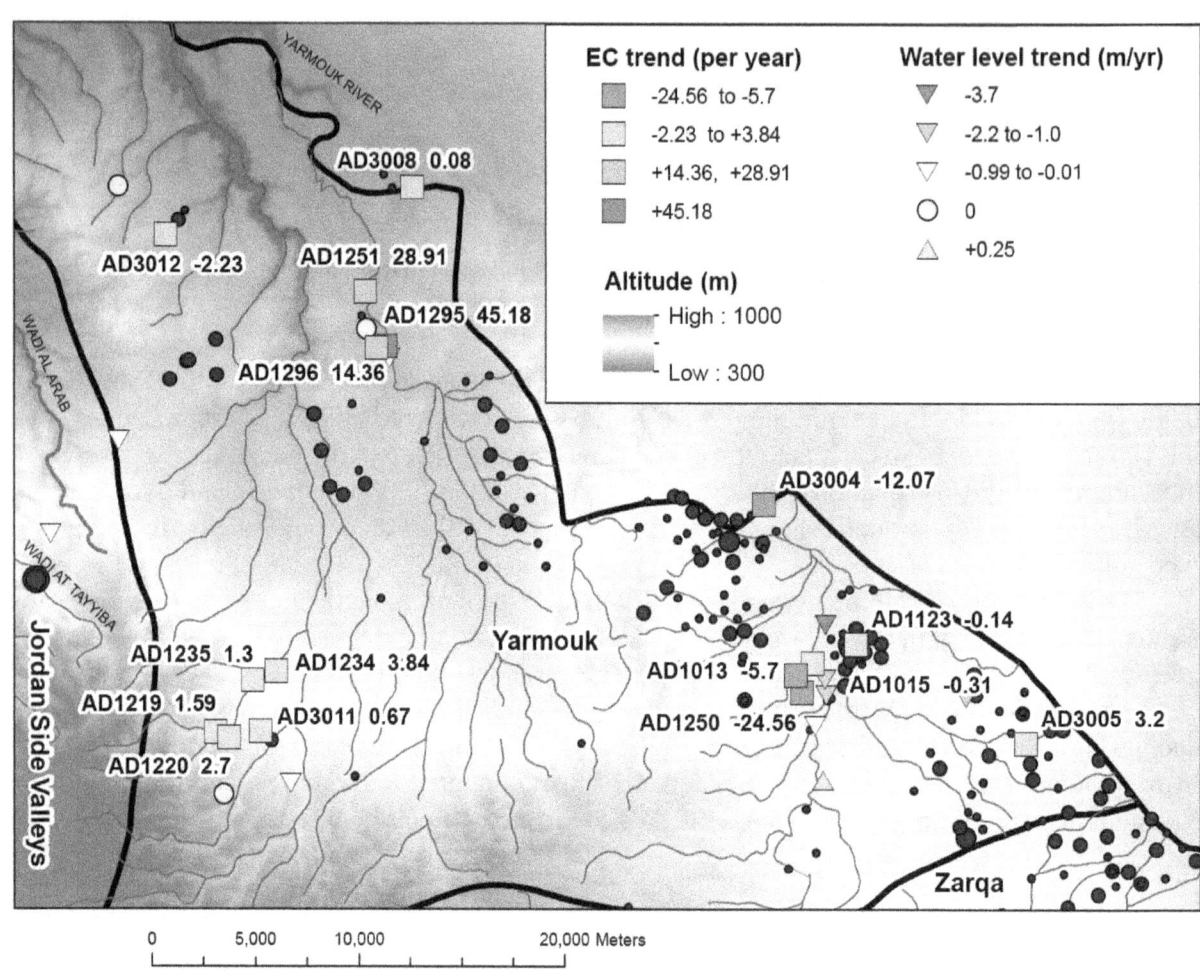

Figure 36. Trends in groundwater electrical conductivity (EC) at selected wells in the Yarmouk groundwater basin, Jordan. The background colors represent land-surface altitude in meters. The long-term groundwater EC trend, in microsiemens per centimeter per year, is shown for all wells with data in 2006 or later. Negative trends indicate decreasing EC. The dark-blue dots are production wells, and the size of the dot represents the annual withdrawal from each well in 2009. Blue lines are stream channels. (Data provided by Ministry of Water and Irrigation, Jordan; m, meters; yr, year)

Zarqa Groundwater Basin

The Zarqa groundwater basin is located in the north-central part of Jordan from Amman in the west to the Syrian border in the northeast (see fig. 1). This groundwater basin is also referred to as "Amman-Zarqa." Groundwater recharge occurs in the western highlands; flow occurs from this area to the lower, central parts of the basin and then towards the Zarqa River (Salameh and Bannayan, 1993). Recharge also occurs in higher altitudes in the northeast, where groundwater flow is generally in the southeastern direction, entering the basin in Jordan. Borgstedt and others (2007) describe the hydrogeology of the eastern part of the basin and note the lack of water-quality data in the Corridor well-field area. Salameh (2004) describes the Zarqa basin hydrogeology and water resources and notes several factors contributing to salinity increases. Salinity in the Zarqa groundwater basin has been studied by numerous authors. Abu-Sharar and Rimawi (1993) characterize the salinity increases in the Dhuleil area and find that salinity is proportional to chloride content and is increasing as a result of over-pumping. They also posit that salinity is derived from dissolution of native rocks and not from irrigation return flow. Margane and others (2009b) provide background information on the hydrogeology of the area and describe groundwater-level and salinity trends in the area.

Groundwater Levels

Groundwater levels were declining in most areas of the Zarqa groundwater basin. A total of 48 monitoring wells had adequate data for analysis of current (2010) groundwater-level trends. Groundwater-level trends were downward at 41 wells, flat at 6 wells, and upward at 1 well (table 12; figs. 37 and 38). The maximum rate of groundwater level decline was -4.2 m/yr, and the rate of groundwater level increase was +0.12 m/yr at the single well with rising levels. The average 2010 groundwater-level trend at monitoring wells in the Zarqa groundwater basin was -1.08 m/yr.

Table 12. Groundwater-level trends and forecast saturated aquifer thicknesses at selected wells in the Zarqa groundwater basin, Jordan. [*Link*]

Table 12 includes three wells that showed steep declines in water levels prior to 2009, but those wells do not have current data (2009 or later) in the database. The current (2010) trend at these wells could not be evaluated without additional measurements. One of these wells without current data, AL3324, previously had the steepest rate of decline in groundwater levels in the Zarqa groundwater basin, -6.3 m/yr, determined on the basis of the long-term linear trend (table 12).

Where aquifer-thickness and well-depth data were available, the groundwater-level trends were used to forecast the saturated thickness in 2030 (table 12; fig. 39) as a percent of the initial saturated thickness, maximum saturated thickness, or the total saturated thickness. In 2030, the average saturated thickness at the monitoring wells in the Zarqa basin was forecast to be 67 percent of the initial or total aquifer saturated thickness. Two monitoring wells were forecast to be dry by 2030.

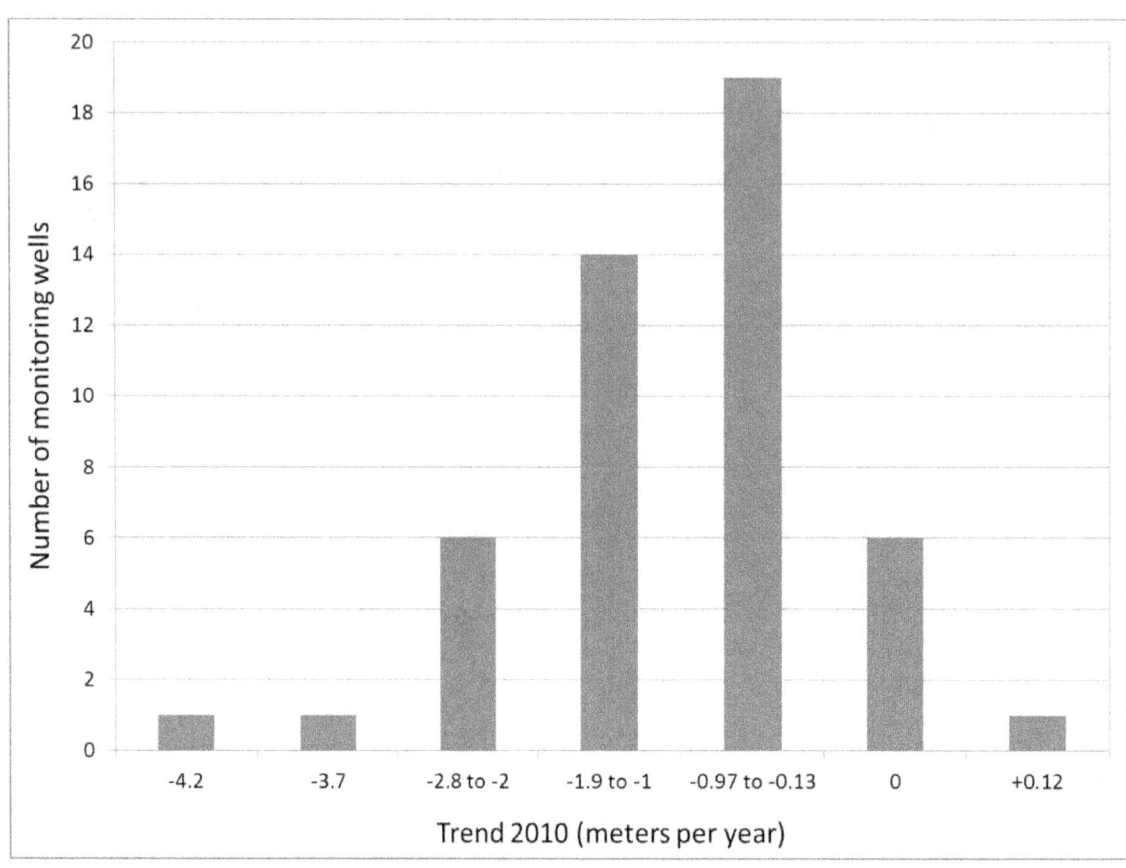

Figure 37. Histogram of groundwater-level trends at selected wells in the Zarqa groundwater basin, Jordan. The groundwater-level trend in 2010, in meters per year, is shown for all monitoring wells with data in 2009 or later. Negative trends indicate declining water levels. Note that the histogram bins are nonuniform. (Data provided by Ministry of Water and Irrigation, Jordan)

Although groundwater levels were falling in most areas of the Zarqa basin, groundwater levels generally were declining most rapidly in areas of high withdrawals. Such areas were in the southwest (near Amman), in the center of the basin, and in the northeast (fig. 38). Monitoring wells are not present in areas of pumping in the eastern part of the basin or in the very northern corner of the basin.

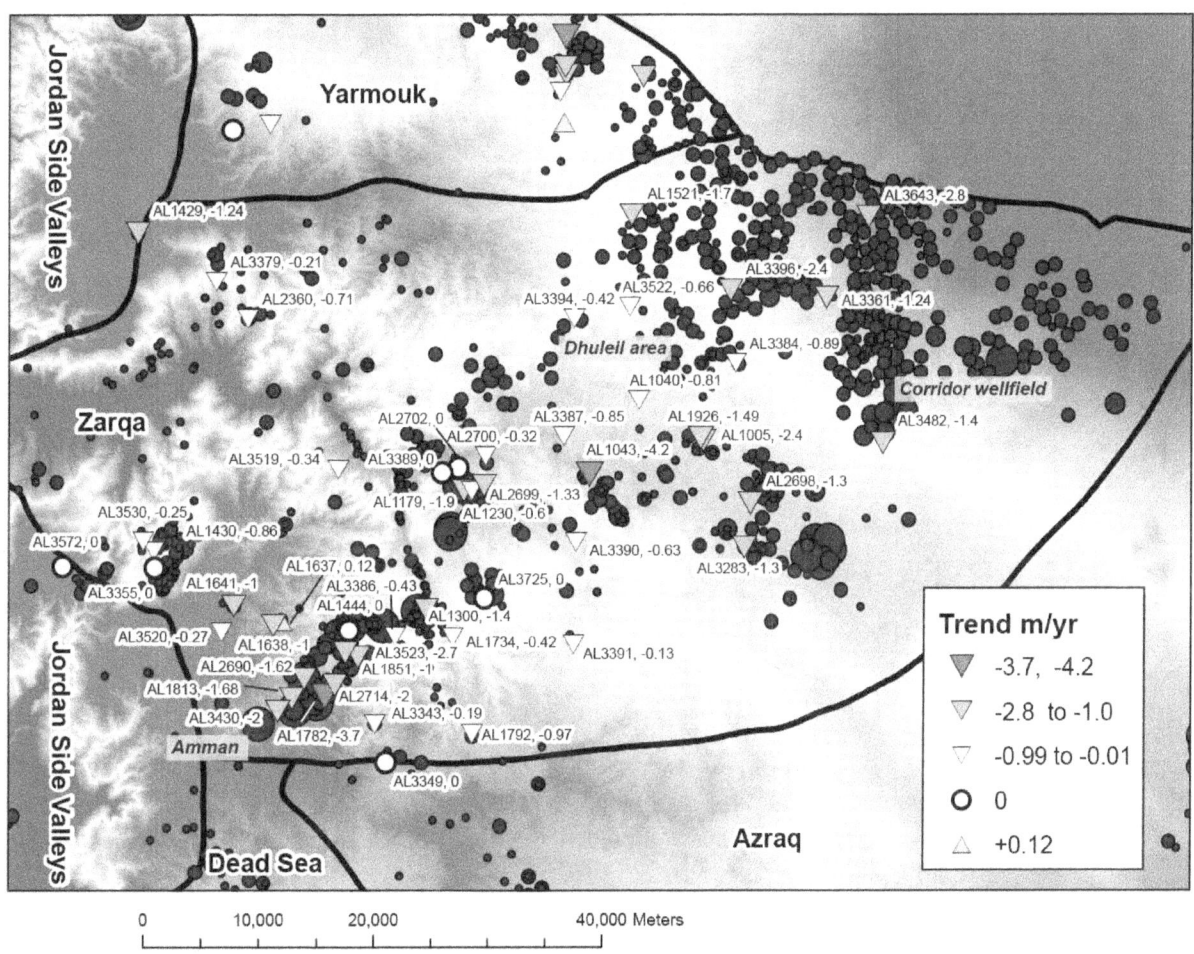

Figure 38. Trends in groundwater levels at selected wells in the Zarqa groundwater basin, Jordan. The background colors represent land-surface altitude in meters, ranging from lower than 400 (brown) to higher than 900 (blue). The groundwater-level trend in 2010, in meters per year, is shown for all monitoring wells with data in 2009 or later. Negative trends indicate declining water levels. The dark-blue dots are production wells, and the size of the dot represents the annual withdrawal from each well in 2009. (Data provided by Ministry of Water and Irrigation, Jordan; m/yr, meters per year)

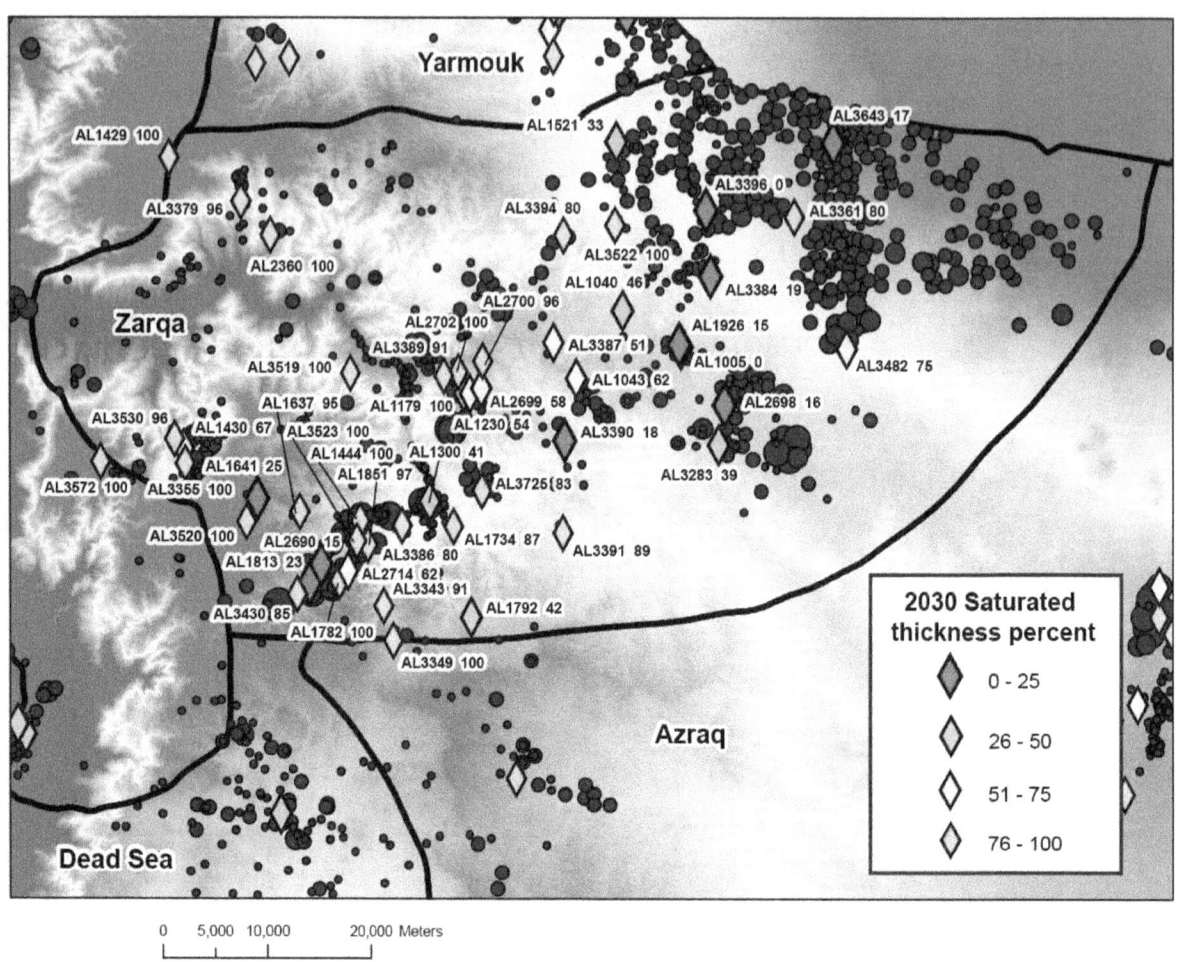

Figure 39. Forecast saturated aquifer thickness in 2030 at selected wells in the Zarqa groundwater basin, Jordan. The background colors represent land-surface altitude in meters, ranging from lower than 400 (brown) to higher than 900 (blue). The dark-blue dots are production wells, and the size of the dot represents the annual withdrawal from each well in 2009. (Data provided by Ministry of Water and Irrigation, Jordan)

The southwestern part of the Zarqa groundwater basin is close to Amman and encompasses the Rusaifah domestic production wells near well AL1444. Of the 17 wells with sufficient data in the area, the trend was downward at 14 wells, upward at 1 well, and flat at 2 wells (fig. 40). In general, groundwater levels declined most rapidly in an area of withdrawals aligned with a wadi draining to the northeast. Smaller declines and, in limited cases, flat or rising groundwater levels occurred at higher altitudes away from withdrawals.

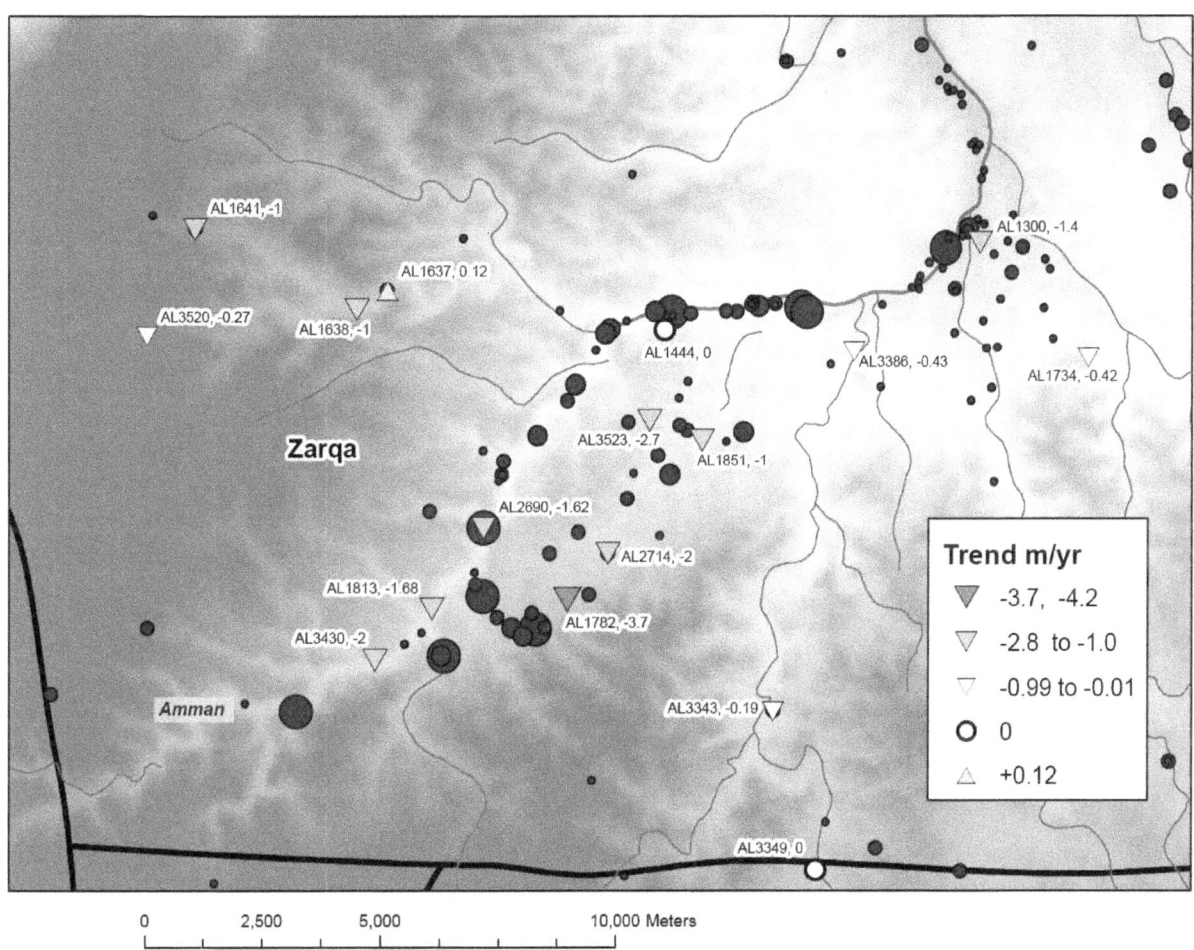

Figure 40. Trends in groundwater levels at selected wells in the Amman area of the Zarqa groundwater basin, Jordan. The background colors represent land-surface altitude in meters, ranging from lower than 400 (brown) to higher than 900 (blue). The groundwater-level trend in 2010, in meters per year, is shown for all wells with data in 2009 or later. Negative trends indicate declining water levels. The dark-blue dots are production wells, and the size of the dot represents the annual withdrawal from each well in 2009. Blue lines are stream channels. (Data provided by Ministry of Water and Irrigation, Jordan; m/yr, meters per year)

The central part of the Zarqa groundwater basin encompasses the Zarqa Industrial Zone near well AL1043 and the Hallabat well field near well AL3283. Of the eight wells with sufficient data, the trend was downward at all eight wells (fig. 41). The highest rate of water-level decline, -4.2 m/yr, was at well AL1043 in the area of the Zarqa Industrial Zone. Monitoring data were not available in the area of highest withdrawals (in 2009), the eastern Hallabat well field (lower right in fig. 41). Margane and others (2009b) describe recent changes in pumping in the area:

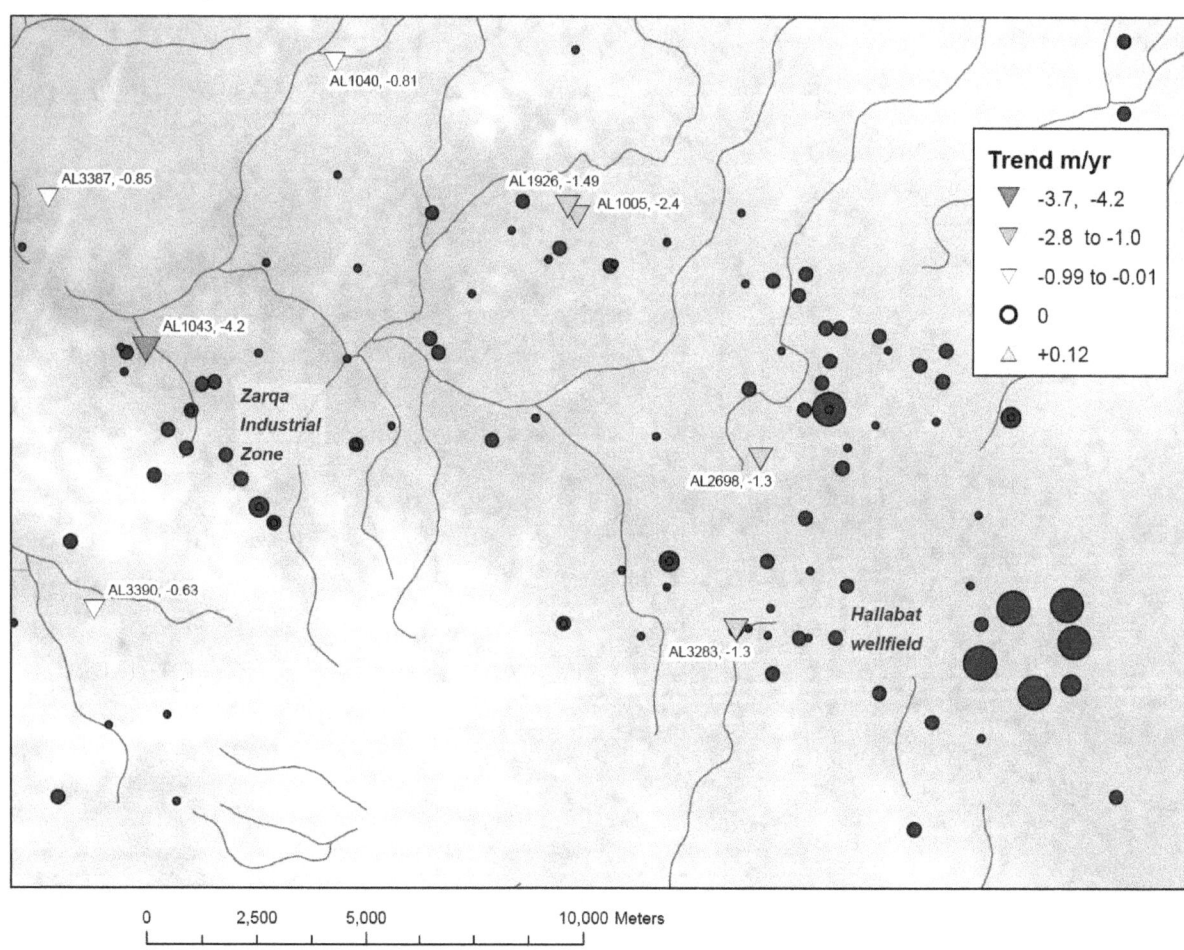

Figure 41. Trends in groundwater levels at selected wells in the central part of the Zarqa groundwater basin, Jordan. The background colors represent land-surface altitude in meters, ranging from lower than 400 (brown) to higher than 900 (blue). The current (2010) groundwater level trend, in meters per year, is shown for all wells with data in 2009 or later. Negative trends indicate declining water levels. The dark-blue dots are production wells, and the size of the dot represents the annual withdrawal from each well in 2009. Blue lines are stream channels. (Data provided by Ministry of Water and Irrigation, Jordan; m/yr, meters per year)

Most wells of the western Hallabat well field are currently not in operation, except wells Hallabat 8, 10 and 14 [AL3285, AL3133, and AL3494]. The main reason for this is that the saturated thickness in the A7/B2 aquifer these wells produce from has become very low. Therefore the yield of all wells has decreased considerably and some wells have run dry. . . . There is a clear decline in the productivity of some western Hallabat wells (AL3494, AL3495, AL3284, AL3306, and AL3127). Therefore the (Water Authority of Jordan) WAJ Directorate of Drilling had drilled new wells to the east (eastern Hallabat well field). The new wells were drilled and tested in 2004.

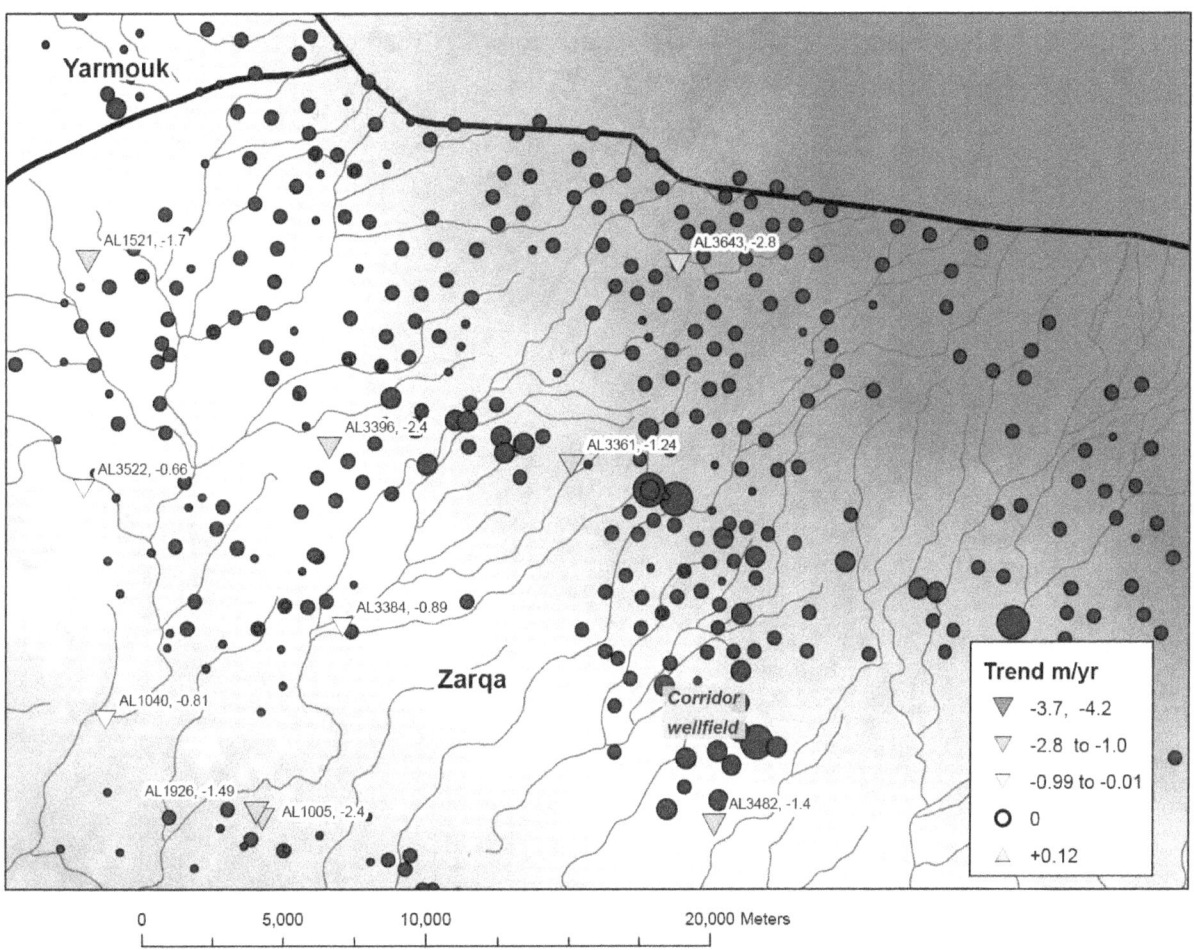

Figure 42.   Trends in groundwater levels at selected wells in the northeastern part of the Zarqa groundwater basin, Jordan. The background colors represent land-surface altitude in meters, ranging from lower than 400 (brown) to higher than 900 (blue). The groundwater-level trend in 2010, in meters per year, is shown for all wells with data in 2009 or later. Negative trends indicate declining water levels. The dark-blue dots are production wells, and the size of the dot represents the annual withdrawal from each well in 2009. Blue lines are stream channels. (Data provided by Ministry of Water and Irrigation, Jordan; m/yr, meters per year)

Groundwater levels also were declining in the heavily pumped northeastern part of the Zarqa groundwater basin (fig. 42). The water-level trend was downward at all 10 wells with adequate current data, and the trend ranged from -0.66 to -2.8 m/yr. There was less variability in the trends in this area than in other areas, possibly as a result of the widely distributed

59

withdrawals. Monitoring wells near each other had similar trends. Monitoring data were not available for the eastern part of this area or for the northern corner of the basin.

This area includes the Corridor well field (southern part of fig. 42) for which well AL3482, "CORODOR 11" (trend -1.4 m/yr) serves as a monitoring well. According to Borgstedt and other (2007), this well was originally drilled as a production well but is used as a monitoring well because of its inadequate yield. Such a well may still be adequate for monitoring long-term water levels and trends, but it may respond slowly to seasonal cycles and shorter transients. The hydrograph for this monitoring well is presented in Appendix F. Pumping occurs to the north of the monitoring well and the Corridor well field; therefore, the trend may be different on the north side of the well field.

Salinity

Groundwater EC trends were variable in the Zarqa groundwater basin (table 13). Current (2009 or later) EC data were available and adequate for 108 wells. Although trends for many wells were flat (-5 to +5 μS/cm/yr) or decreasing EC, 58 percent of the wells had increasing EC trend (fig. 43). The average trend was +15.26 μS/cm/yr, and the median was +8.80 μS/cm/yr.

Table 13. Groundwater electrical-conductivity trends at selected wells in the Zarqa groundwater basin, Jordan. [*Link*]

Figure 43. Histogram of trends in groundwater electrical conductivity (EC) in the Zarqa groundwater basin, Jordan. The long-term EC trend, in microsiemens per centimeter per year, is shown for all wells with data in 2009 or later. Note that the histogram bins are nonuniform. (Data provided by Ministry of Water and Irrigation, Jordan)

The variability in EC was large at many wells, and the linear trend regression R^2 ranged from 0.0 to 0.97. In general, the trend estimates are considered highly uncertain because of the variable strength of linear fits to the data, as measured by R^2, and the small number of EC measurements at many locations (table 13). The quality of the fit of the linear trend over time and the scatter of data around this trend line are graphically illustrated for all wells studied in Appendix F.

Groundwater EC trends were spatially variable in the Zarqa groundwater basin (figs. 44–49). The causes of the variability in trends, and current EC values, are likely related to local hydrogeologic and flow conditions. Several areas, including areas of distributed pumping in the eastern part of the basin and the Corridor well field, did not have adequate EC data for an evaluation of current trends. Groundwater EC was increasing substantially in pumping centers at lower altitudes in the central part of the Zarqa basin (figs. 44, 47, 48, and 49). These low areas are the natural discharge areas for groundwater flow through the basin (Salameh, 1996), and water discharging in this area has a relatively long residence time in the basin. In contrast, EC trends were more variable, and showed more gradual increases, in areas of higher altitude to the east and west (figs. 44–46) and in areas with low withdrawals. The high altitudes, especially to the west, are areas of active groundwater recharge of freshwater and substantial leakage from municipal water and sewage systems (Salameh, 1996).

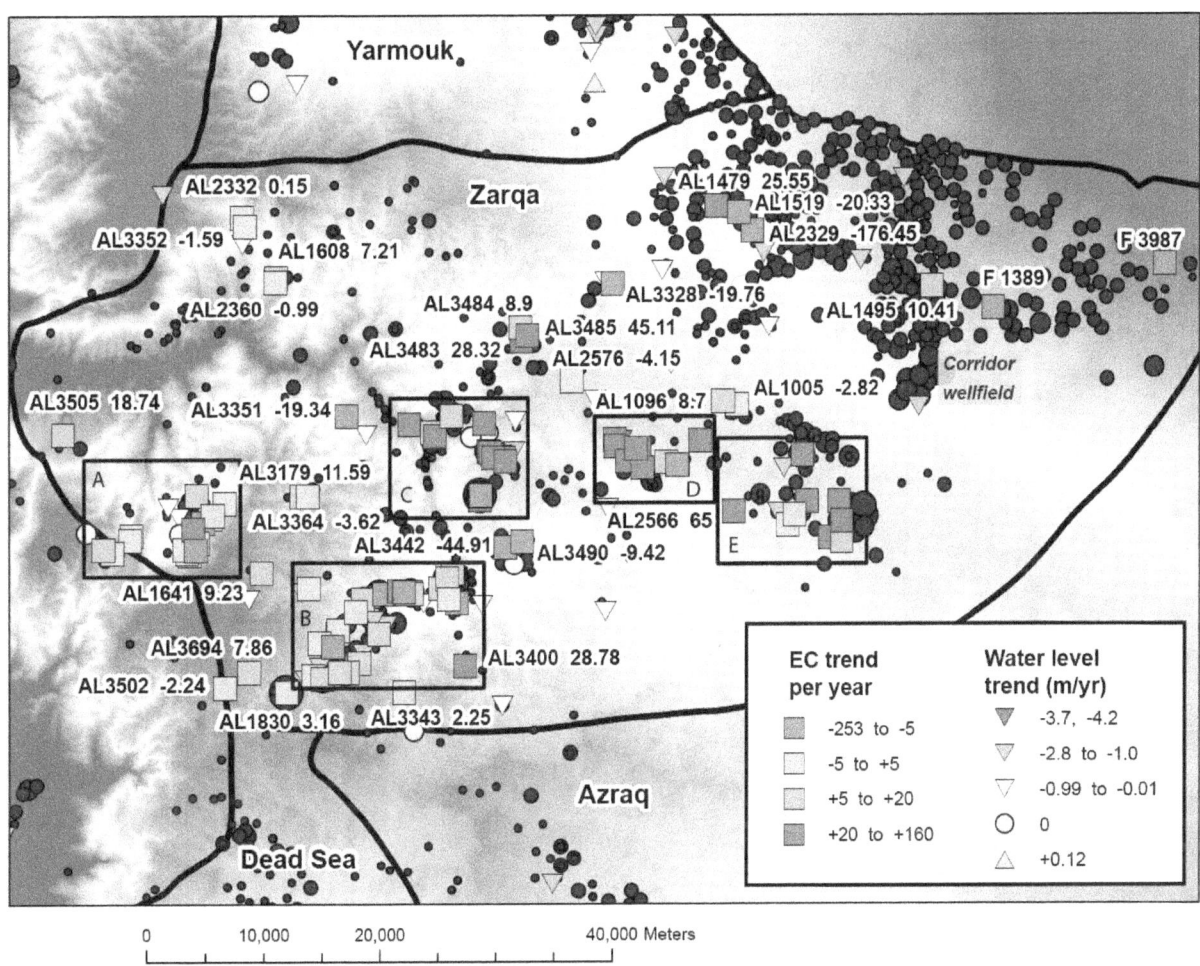

Figure 44. Trends in groundwater electrical conductivity (EC) at selected wells in the Zarqa groundwater basin, Jordan. The background colors represent land-surface altitude in meters, ranging from lower than 300 (brown) to higher than 1000 (blue). The long-term groundwater EC trend, in microsiemens per centimeter per year, is shown for all wells with data in 2009 or later. Negative trends indicate decreasing EC. The triangles and light-green circles represent water-level trends (see fig. 39). The dark-blue dots are production wells, and the size of the dot represents the annual withdrawal from each well in 2009. Detailed views of the areas in the labeled boxes are shown in other figures (for example, area of box "A" is shown in fig. 45). (Data provided by Ministry of Water and Irrigation, Jordan; m/yr, meters per year)

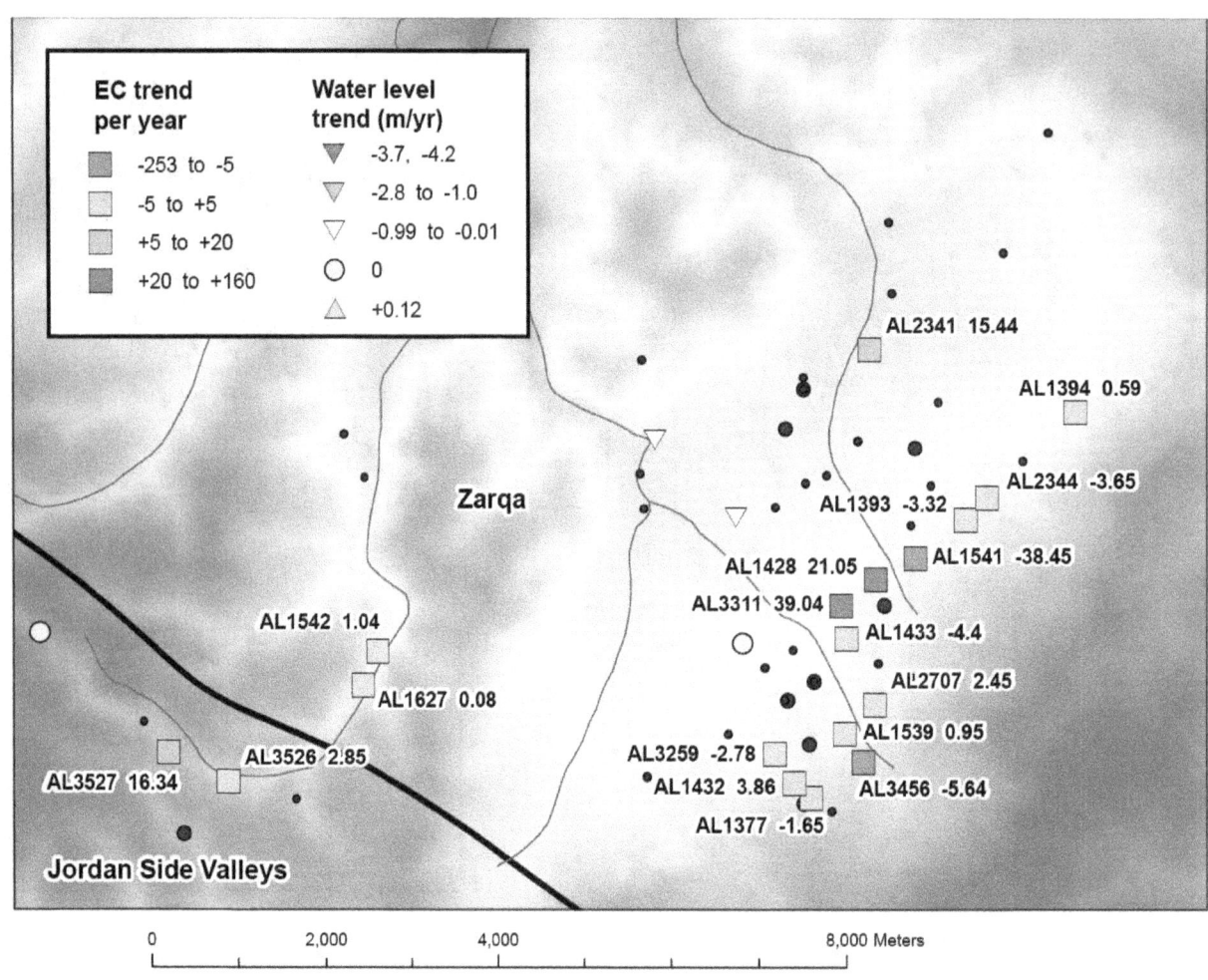

Figure 45. Trends in groundwater electrical conductivity (EC) at selected wells in the western part of the Zarqa groundwater basin, Jordan (box "A" in fig. 44). The background colors represent land-surface altitude in meters, ranging from lower than 300 (brown) to higher than 1000 (blue). The long-term EC trend, in microsiemens per centimeter per year, is shown for all wells with data in 2009 or later by colored squares. Negative trends indicate decreasing EC. Triangles and light-green circles represent water-level trends (see fig. 39). The dark-blue dots are production wells, and the size of the dot represents the annual withdrawal from each well in 2009. Blue lines are stream channels. (Data provided by Ministry of Water and Irrigation, Jordan; m/yr, meters per year)

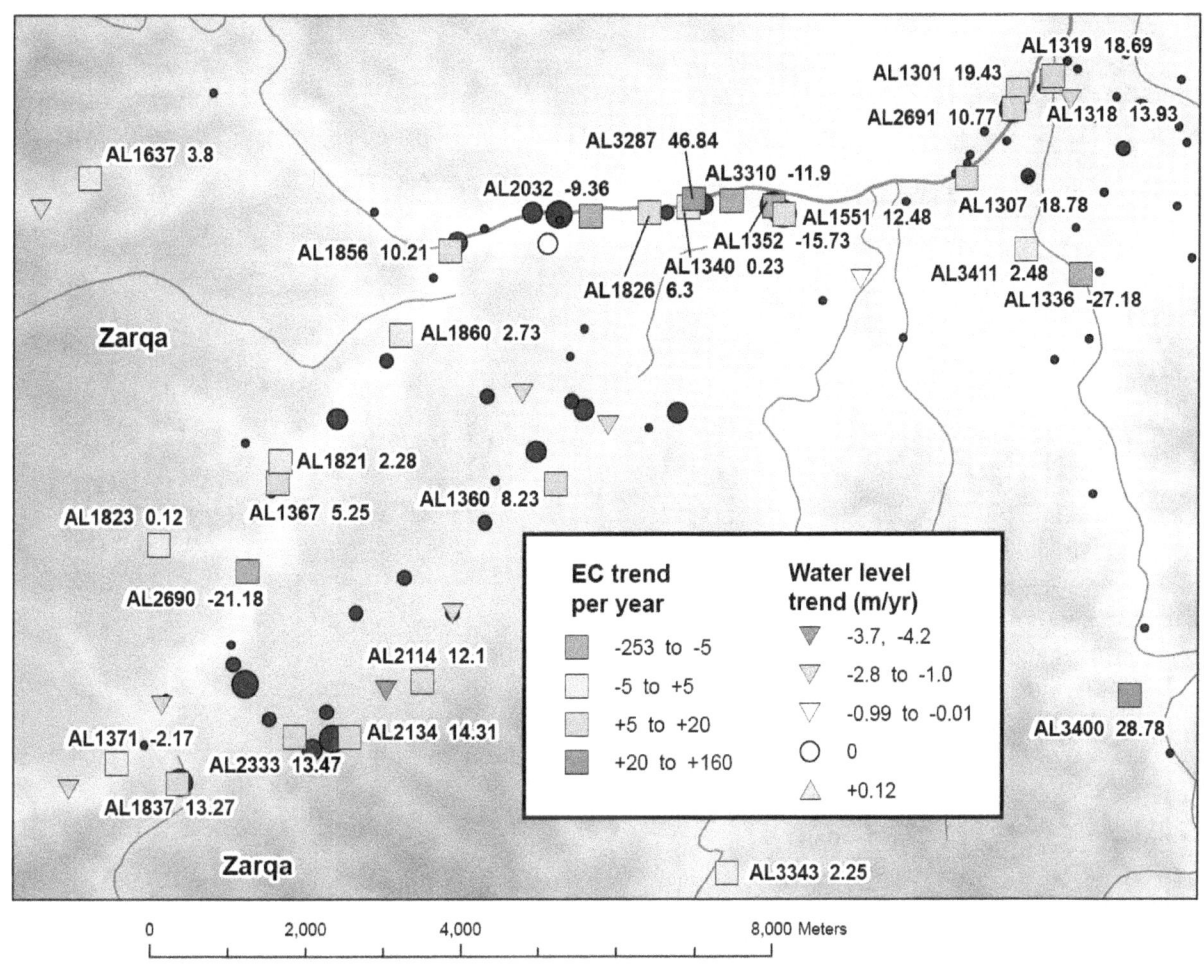

Figure 46. Trends in groundwater electrical conductivity (EC) at selected wells in the southwestern part of Zarqa groundwater basin, Jordan (box "B" in fig. 44). The background colors represent land-surface altitude in meters, ranging from lower than 300 (brown) to higher than 1000 (blue). The long-term EC trend, in microsiemens per centimeter per year, is shown for all wells with data in 2009 or later. Negative trends indicate decreasing EC. Triangles and light-green circles represent water-level trends (see figs. 39 and 40). The dark-blue dots are production wells, and the size of the dot represents the annual withdrawal from each well in 2009. Blue lines are stream channels. (Data provided by Ministry of Water and Irrigation, Jordan; m/yr, meters per year)

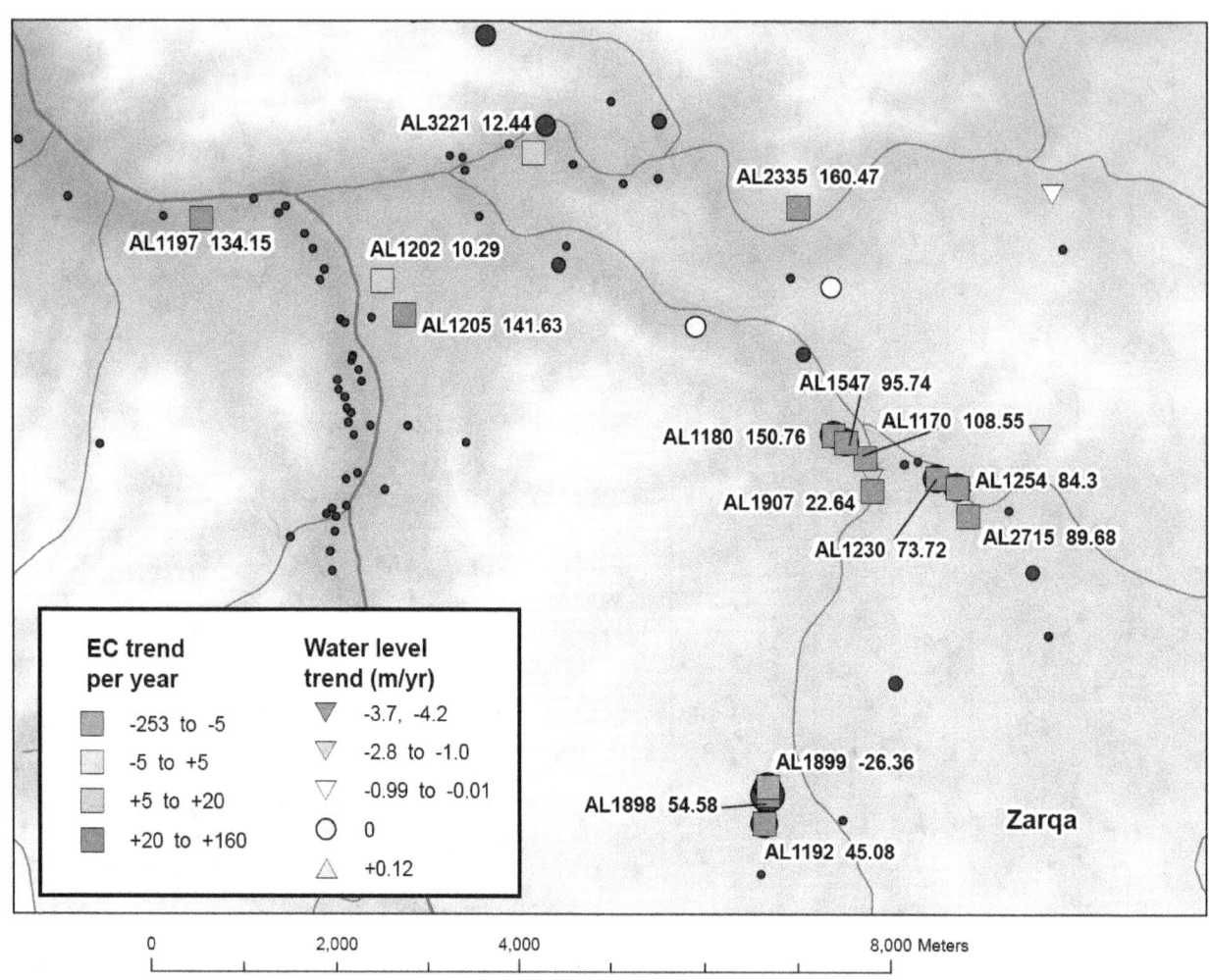

Figure 47. Trends in groundwater electrical conductivity (EC) at selected wells near the Zarqa River channel in the central part of the Zarqa groundwater basin, Jordan (box "C" in fig. 44). The background colors represent land-surface altitude in meters, ranging from lower than 300 (brown) to higher than 1000 (blue). The long-term EC trend, in microsiemens per centimeter per year, is shown for all wells with data in 2009 or later. Negative trends indicate decreasing EC. Triangles and light-green circles are water-level trends (see fig. 39). The dark-blue dots are production wells, and the size of the dot represents the annual withdrawal from each well in 2009. Blue lines are stream channels. (Data provided by Ministry of Water and Irrigation, Jordan; m/yr, meters per year)

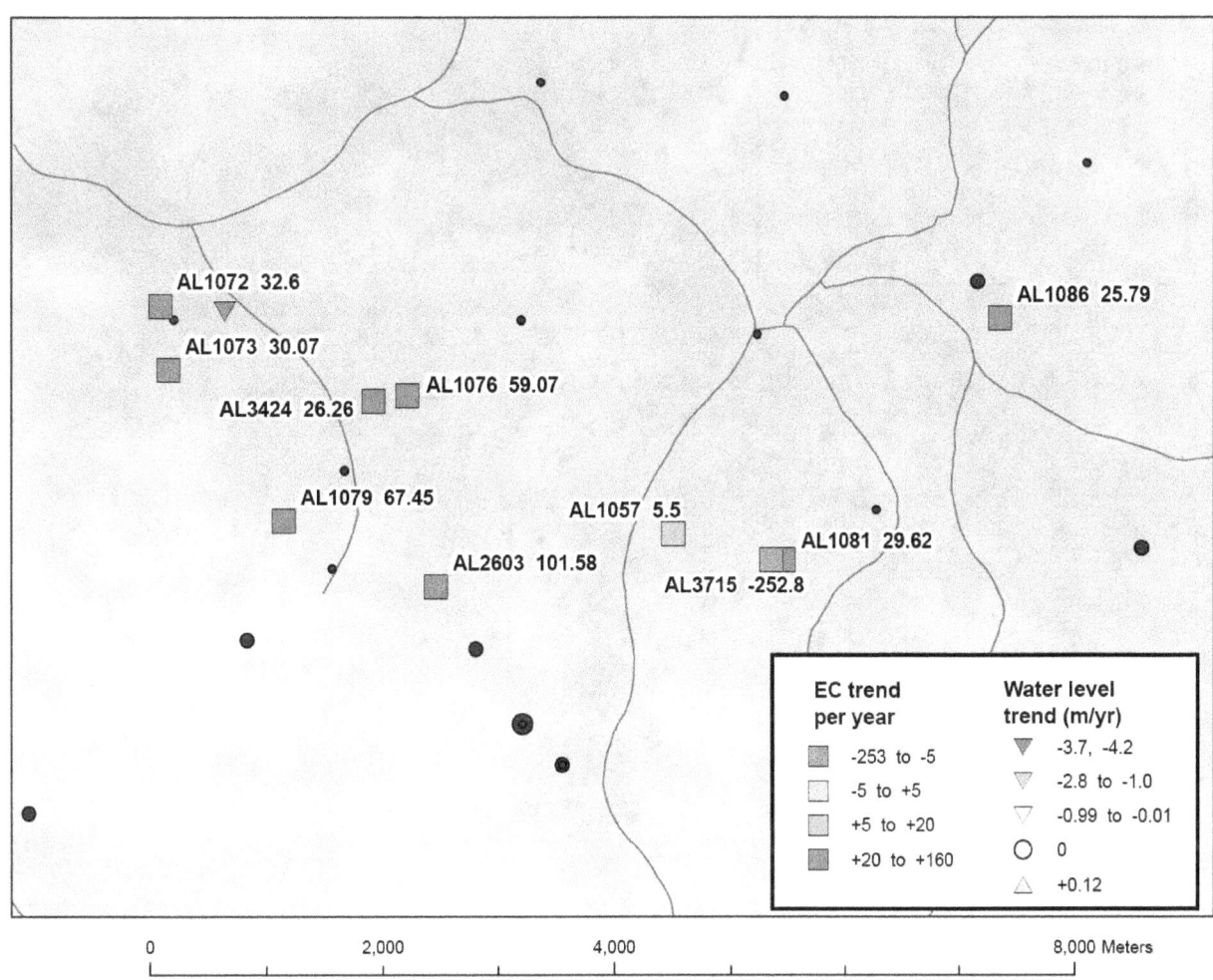

Figure 48. Trends in groundwater electrical conductivity (EC) at selected wells in the Dhuleil area of the Zarqa groundwater basin, Jordan (box "D" in fig. 44). The background colors represent land-surface altitude in meters, ranging from lower than 300 (brown) to higher than 1000 (blue). The long-term EC trend, in microsiemens per centimeter per year, is shown for all wells with data in 2009 or later. Negative trends indicate decreasing EC. Triangles are water-level trends (see fig. 41). The dark-blue dots are production wells, and the size of the dot represents the annual withdrawal from each well in 2009. Blue lines are stream channels. (Data provided by Ministry of Water and Irrigation, Jordan; m/yr, meters per year)

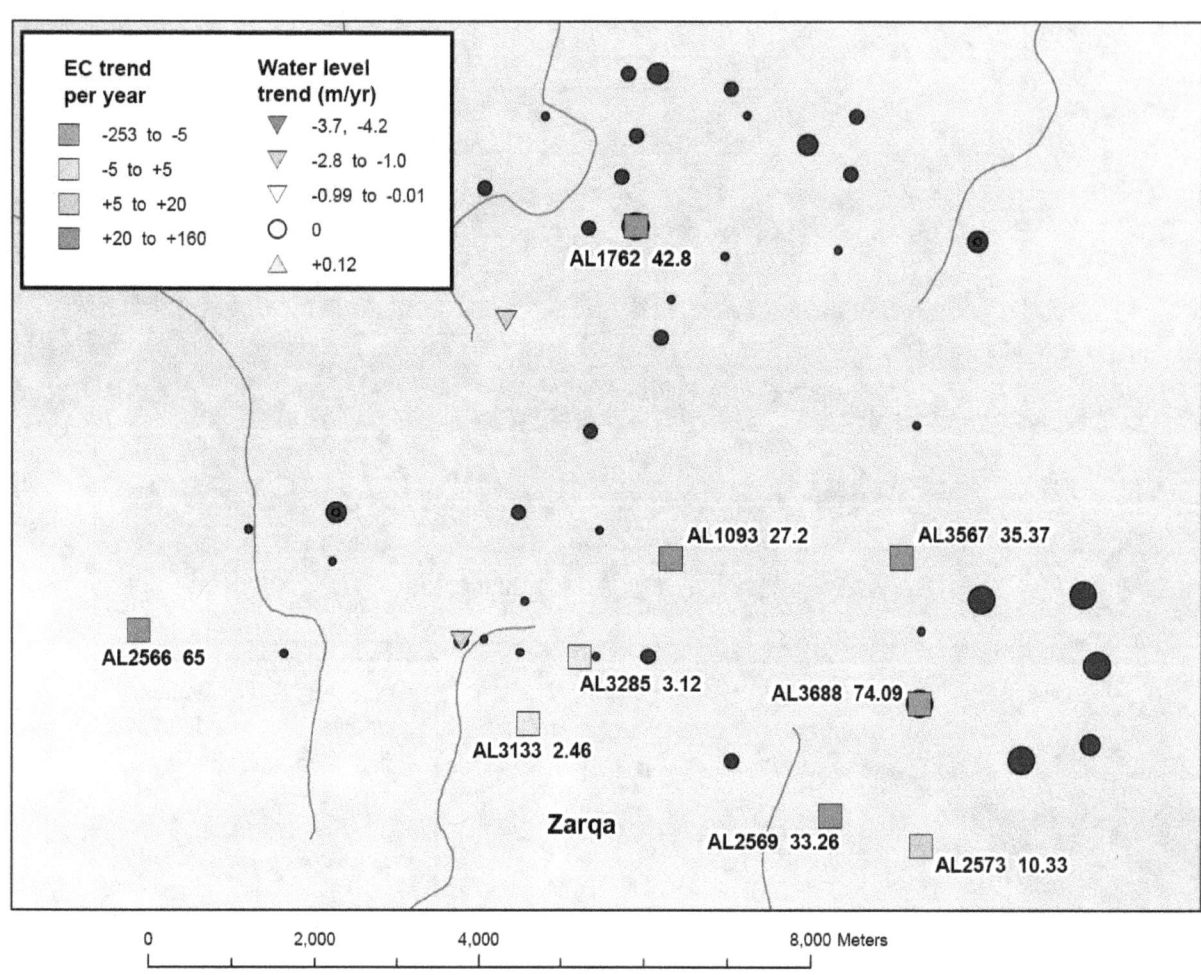

Figure 49.   Trends in groundwater electrical conductivity (EC) at selected wells in the Hallabat well field area of the Zarqa groundwater basin, Jordan (box "E" in fig. 44). The background colors represent land-surface altitude in meters, ranging from lower than 300 (brown) to higher than 1000 (blue). The long-term EC trend, in microsiemens per centimeter per year, is shown for all wells with data in 2009 or later. Negative trends indicate decreasing EC. Triangles represent the water-level trends (see fig. 39). The dark-blue dots are production wells, and the size of the dot represents the annual withdrawal from each well in 2009. Blue lines are stream channels. (Data provided by Ministry of Water and Irrigation, Jordan; m/yr, meters per year)

Summary and Conclusions

Trends in groundwater levels and salinity in six groundwater basins in Jordan were characterized by using linear regression for well-monitoring data collected by the Jordan Ministry of Water and Irrigation (MWI) from 1971 to 2011. Trends in groundwater levels were used to forecast the percentage of aquifer saturated thickness in 2030.

Groundwater levels

The groundwater-level trends in 2010, averaged for each basin, range from 0 to -1.9 meters per year (m/yr) (table 14). Four of the six basins had an average trend of approximately -1.0 m/yr, yielding a forecast average water-level decline of about 20 meters by 2030 in these basins. Hammad groundwater basin had no trend, on average, and the average groundwater-level decline was greatest in the Jordan Side Valleys basin, at -1.9 m/yr, and thus the forecast average groundwater-level decline in this basin was about 38 meters by 2030. The maximum current rate of decline at an individual well in each basin ranged from -0.2 to -9 m/yr. The forecast average saturated thickness in 2030 ranged from 61 to 98 percent (table 14). The average saturated thickness was forecast to remain relatively unchanged in the Hammad basin, whereas all other basins were forecast to have substantial declines in saturated thickness. Some locations in three of the basins were forecast to have zero saturated thickness by 2030.

Water levels were declining in most wells in Jordan (figs. 50 and 51). (Hammad basin is not shown; see separate section on Hammad water levels.) The fastest rates of groundwater-level decline occurred near major pumping centers. Water-level trends were variable in that wells with rapid water-level declines were located near wells with modest declines, no trends, or small rises in water levels. Explanation of these differences may be related to the different depths or aquifers that the wells penetrate, but these local conditions were not explored in this study. Adequate data were not available to evaluate the groundwater-level trends in some areas of heavy withdrawals, such as the eastern parts of the Yarmouk and Zarqa basins (fig. 50).

Table 14. Summary of groundwater-level trends in 2010 and forecast saturated aquifer thicknesses in 2030 in six groundwater basins, Jordan.

Groundwater basin	Number of wells	Groundwater level trend 2010 (meters per year)		Forecast 2030 saturated thickness (percent)		Number of wells dry in 2030
		Average	Maximum	Average	Minimum	
Azraq	15	-0.8	-2.3	69	14	0
Dead Sea	30	-0.8	-9	61	0	3
Hammad	4	0	-0.2	98	93	0
Jordan Side Valleys	9	-1.9	-9	64	20	0
Yarmouk	11	-1.1	-3.7	66	0	1
Zarqa	48	-1.1	-4.2	67	0	2

Key findings – Groundwater levels

☐ Data quality was very good, but monitoring data were not available for some areas.

☐ Groundwater levels continued to decline about -1 m/yr in groundwater basins with large withdrawals.

☐ In most cases, rates of decline were constant or increasing (faster decline).

☐ If these rates of decline continue, average saturated aquifer thicknesses were forecast to decline 30 to 40 percent by 2030.

☐ Saturated aquifer thickness was forecast to be zero by 2030 in 5 percent of the locations evaluated.

☐ Some shallow wells that do not fully penetrate the aquifer will likely go dry, and go dry more frequently where rates of decline are increasing.

☐ Less water is stored in aquifers in Jordan as groundwater levels decline.

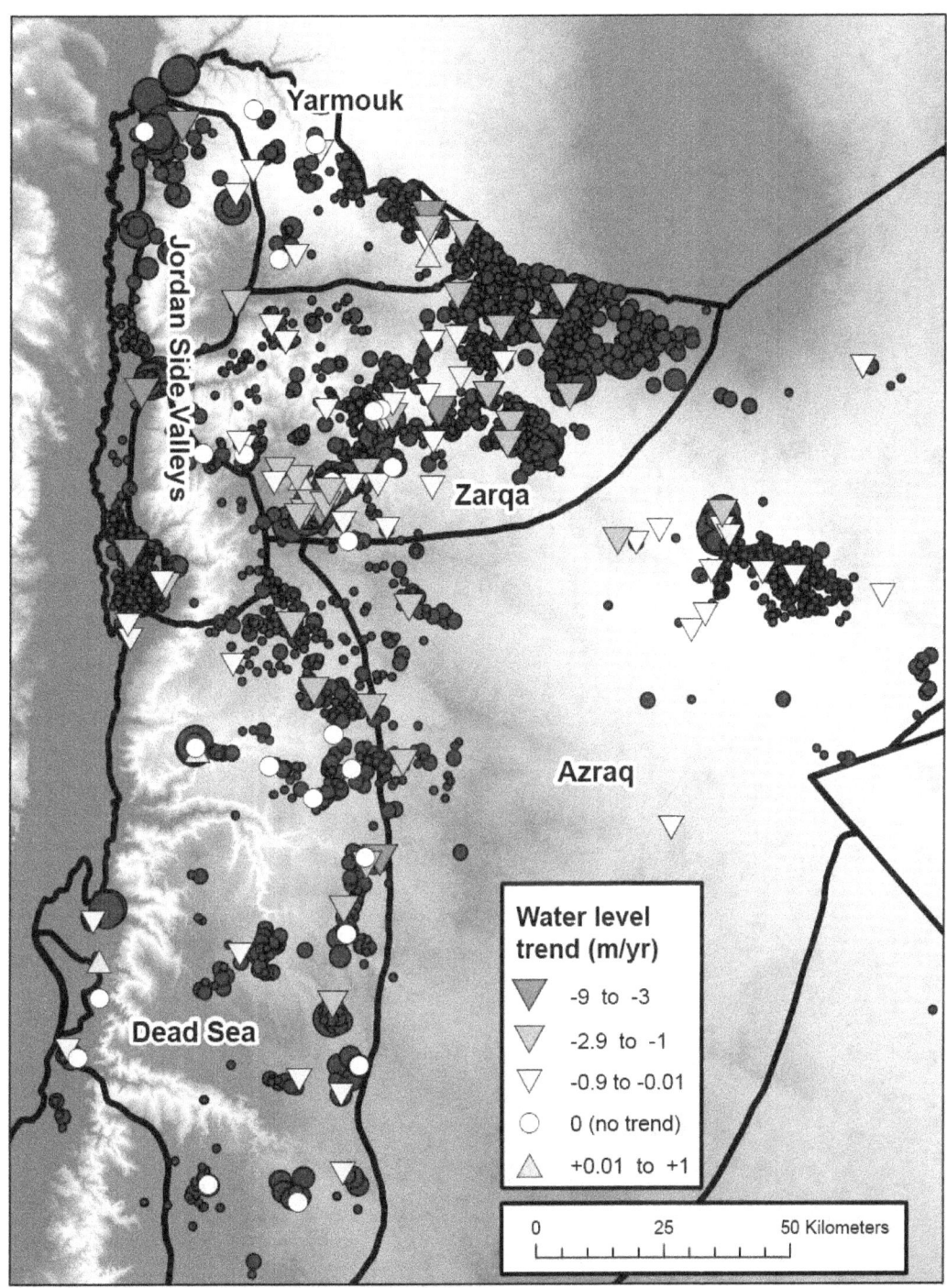

Figure 50. Trends in groundwater levels at selected wells in Jordan. The background colors represent land-surface altitude in meters, ranging from lower than 0 (brown) to higher than 1000 (blue). The groundwater-level trend in 2010, in meters per year, is shown for all wells with data in 2009 or later. Negative trends indicate declining water levels. The dark-blue dots are production wells, and the size of the dot represents the annual withdrawal from each well in 2009. (Data provided by Ministry of Water and Irrigation, Jordan; m/yr, meters per year)

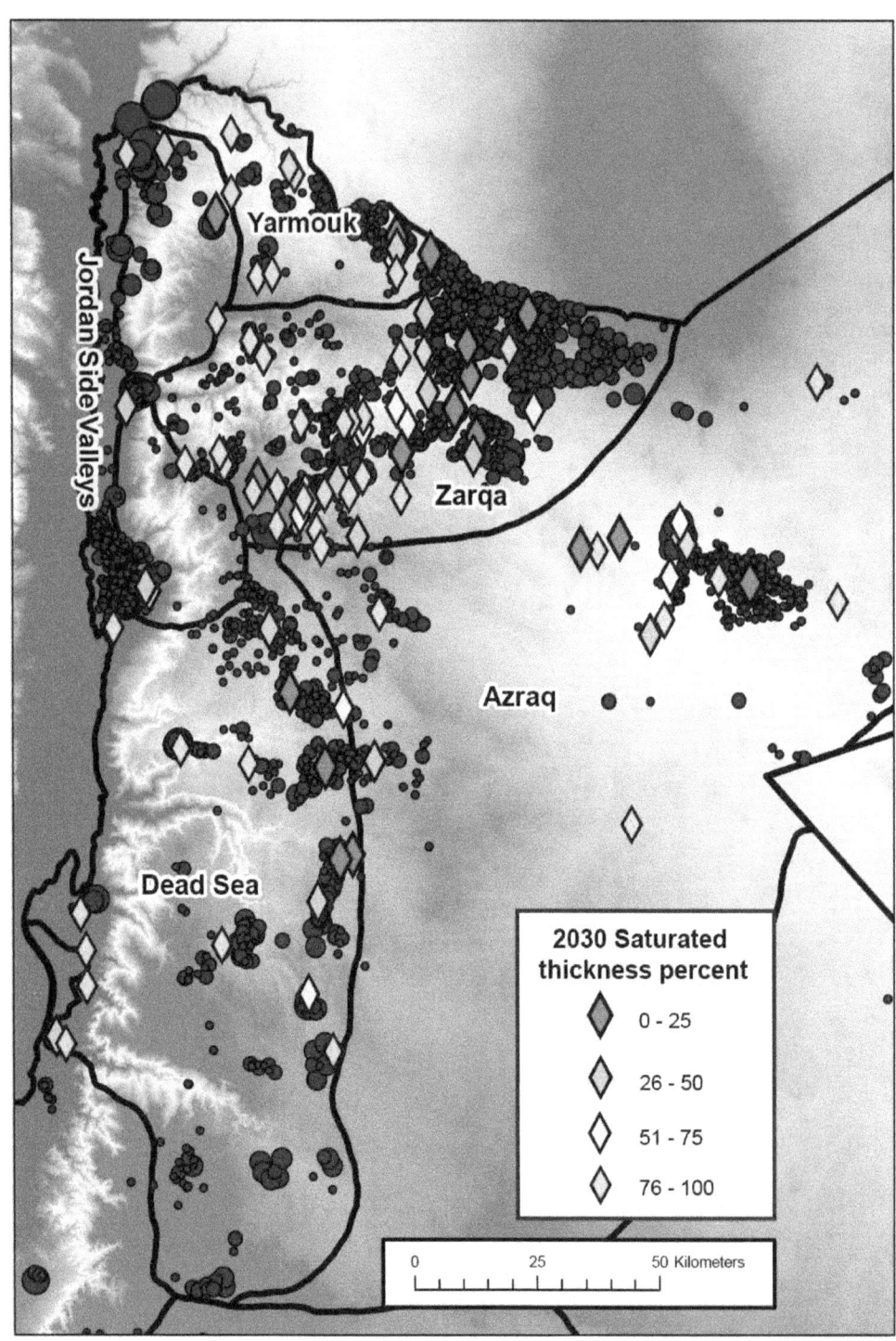

Figure 51.   Forecast saturated aquifer thickness in 2030 at selected wells in Jordan. The background colors represent land-surface altitude in meters, ranging from lower than 0 (brown) to higher than 1000 (blue). The saturated thickness, as a percent (0-100) of total or maximum saturated thickness, is shown for all wells with data in 2009 or later and with aquifer information. The dark-blue dots are production wells, and the size of the dot represents the annual withdrawal from each well in 2009. (Data provided by Ministry of Water and Irrigation, Jordan)

Salinity

Groundwater electrical conductivity (EC) was used as a surrogate for salinity. The long-term linear trend in groundwater EC, averaged by basin, ranged from -2.8 to +27 (table 15). The Jordan Side Valleys basin was the only basin with an average trend of decreasing EC. A trend of + / - 5 microsiemens per centimeter per year (μS/cm/yr) was considered flat (no substantial trend) for summary purposes. The proportion of wells where the trend was increasing EC, greater than +5 μS/cm/yr, ranged from 19 to 66 percent, with the highest percentage in the arid Hammad basin. (Note that groundwater levels were not declining rapidly in the Hammad basin, and only six wells have current EC data defined as "current.") The heavily pumped Zarqa basin had many wells with current EC data, including the second highest EC value, and had the second highest average rate of EC increase; the EC trend was greater than +5 μS/cm/yr for 58 percent of the wells studied.

Groundwater EC trends were highly variable in Jordan (fig. 52; Hammad basin is not shown. See separate section on Hammad EC trends.) Most wells with rapidly increasing EC are located at lower altitudes in the basins, which represent discharge areas, away from freshwater recharge. As noted by Salemeh (1996), "Generally, the water salinity increases in the direction of groundwater flow; from the areas adjacent to the recharge areas to the discharge areas." For example, trends were rapidly increasing EC in the central part of the Zarqa basin and the oasis area of the Azraq basin. Likewise, a few wells near the Dead Sea had trends of rapidly increasing EC. Trends were variable in that wells with rapid EC increases are near wells with flat or decreasing EC trends. These differences may be related to the different depths or aquifers that the wells penetrate, but these local conditions were not explored in this study. Salinity may also be affected by local irrigation and wastewater leakage. Adequate data were not available to evaluate the groundwater EC trends in some areas of heavy withdrawals (fig. 52).

Table 15. Summary of groundwater electrical-conductivity trends in six groundwater basins, Jordan.
[μS/cm, microsiemens per centimeter; yr, year; %, percent]

Groundwater basin	Number of wells	Most recent electrical conductivity (μS/cm)	Long-term linear trend (μS/cm/yr)	Percentage of wells with trend greater than +/- 5 μS/cm/yr	
		Average	Average	% +	% -
Azraq	25	1290	+ 27	26	20
Dead Sea	28	1180	+ 10.5	43	25
Hammad	6	1590	+ 4.9	66	16
Jordan Side Valleys	24	989	- 2.8	19	25
Yarmouk	16	990	+ 3.5	19	19
Zarqa	106	1487	+ 16	58	14

Key findings – Groundwater salinity

☐ Salinity data were much more variable and sparse than water-level data, thus the estimated trends have high uncertainty.

☐ Salinity was not increasing rapidly in most wells, except in Zarqa and Hammad basins.

☐ Salinity was increasing in lower parts of basins, in discharge areas, and generally near heavy withdrawals.

☐ Changes in pumping patterns or blending necessitated by salinity will likely occur more frequently in the future where salinity is increasing.

☐ Groundwater-level declines did not necessarily imply salinity increases; geologic setting, amount of recharge, and position relative to recharge and discharge areas were important factors contributing to high salinity and increasing salinity trends.

☐ Less freshwater will be available from aquifers in Jordan as groundwater salinity increases.

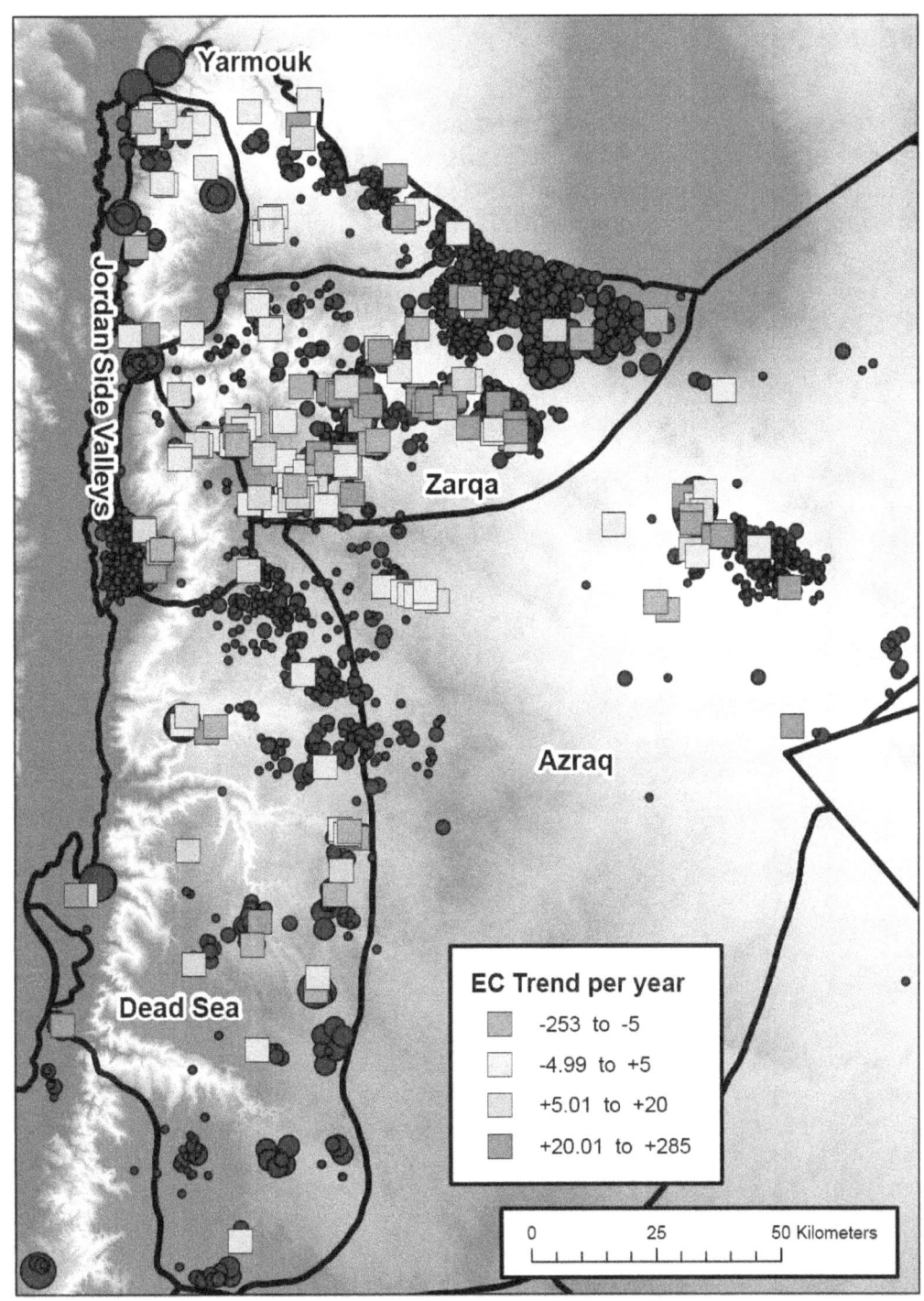

Figure 52. Trends in groundwater electrical-conductivity (EC) at selected wells in Jordan. The background colors represent land-surface altitude in meters, ranging from lower than 0 (brown) to higher than 1000 (blue). The long-term EC trend, in microsiemens per centimeter per year, is shown for all monitoring wells with data in 2009 (2006 in Azraq and Jordan Side Valleys) or later. The dark-blue dots are production wells, and the size of the dot represents the annual withdrawal from each well in 2009. (Data provided by Ministry of Water and Irrigation, Jordan)

Acknowledgments

The authors are grateful for the technical guidance and support of Maysoon Zoubi, former Secretary General of the Ministry of Water and Irrigation (MWI), Jordan. We are also grateful for technical background information and data provided by Tobias El-Fahem and Ibraheem Hamdan of the MWI/Bundesanstalt für Geowissenschaften und Rohstoffe (BGR) Water Aspects in Landuse Planning project. Ali Breazat and Ali Hayajneh, MWI, contributed to groundwater-level trends analysis for wells in Azraq basin. Linda Zarr, USGS, contributed to data analysis. The report was reviewed by Michaela Johnson, Dennis Low, and Ruth Larkins, USGS.

References Cited

Abu-El-Sha'r, W.Y., and Hatamleh, R.I., 2007, Using Modflow and MT3D groundwater flow and transport models as a management tool for the Azraq groundwater system: Jordan Journal of Civil Engineering, v. 1, no. 2, p. 153–172. (Also available at *http://elearning.just.edu.jo/jjce/issues/paper.php?p=19.pdf.*)

Abu-Jaber, Nizar, and Kharabsheh, Alaa, 2008, Ground water origin and movement in the upper Yarmouk Basin, Northern Jordan: Environmental Geology, v. 54, no. 7, p. 1355–1365, Doi: 10.1007/s00254-007-0917-1. (Also available at *http://dx.doi.org/10.1007/s00254-007-0917-1.*)

Abu-Sharar, Taleb M., and Rimawi, Omar, 1993, Water chemistry of the Dhuleil aquifer (Jordan) as influenced by long-term pumpage: Journal of Hydrology, v. 149, no. 1–4, p. 49–66, ISSN 0022-1694, DOI: 10.1016/0022-1694(93)90099-U (Also available at *http://www.sciencedirect.com/science/article/B6V6C-487F7KN-CX/2/5d5e86b7233a76245d3914d24cd70594.*)

Al-Momani, M., Kilani, S., El-Naqa, A., and Amro, H., 2006, Isotope response to hydrological systems for long-term exploitation, Case of Azraq Basin, Jordan, *in* International Atomic Energy Agency, Isotopic assessment of long term groundwater exploitation, IAEA-TECDOC-1507, Vienna, Austria, p. 177–211.(Also available at *http://www-pub.iaea.org/MTCD/publications/PDF/te_1507_web/PDF/TE_1507.pdf.*)

Associates in Rural Development, Inc. (ARD), 2000, Outline hydrogeology of the Amman-Zarqa basin: Unpublished report for Jordan Ministry of Water and Irrigation and U.S. Agency for International Development, USAID/ARD Contract No. LAG-I-00-99-00018-0, Amman, 14 p., accessed August 28, 2012 at *http://pdf.usaid.gov/pdf_docs/PNACP586.pdf.*

Bajjali, William, 2008, Evaluation of groundwater in a three-aquifer system in Ramtha area, Jordan: recharge mechanisms, hydraulic relationship and geochemical evolution: Hydrogeology Journal, v. 16, no. 6, p. 1193–1205, Doi: 10.1007/s10040-008-0284-3. (Also available at *http://dx.doi.org/10.1007/s10040-008-0284-3.*)

Bajjali, W., and Abu-Jaber, N., 2001, Climatological signals of the paleogroundwater in Jordan: Journal of Hydrology, v. 243, no. 1–2, p. 133–147, Doi: 10.1016/s0022-1694(00)00409-1.

Batayneh, A.T., Al-Momani, I.F., Jaradat, R.A., Awawdeh, M.M., Rawashdeh, A.N.M., and Ta'any, R.A, 2008, Weathering processes effects on the chemistry of the main springs of the Yarmouk basin, north Jordan: Journal of Environmental Hydrology, v. 16, 11 p., accessed November 19, 2012 at *http://www.hydroweb.com/journal-hydrology-2008-paper-20.html* .

Borgstedt, Ariane, Margane, Armin, Subah, Ali, Hajali, Zakkaria, Almomani, Thair, Khalifa, Nidal, Jaber, Ayman, and Hamdan, Ibraheem, 2007, Delineation of groundwater protection zones for the Corridor well field: BGR & MWI Technical Cooperation Project, Groundwater Resources Management, Technical Report no. 8, 173 p., Ministry of Water and Irrigation, Amman.

Dottridge, Jane, and Abu Jaber, Nizar, 1999, Groundwater resources and quality in northeastern Jordan: Safe yield and sustainability: Applied Geography, v. 19, no. 4, p. 313–323, (Also available at *http://www.sciencedirect.com/science/article/B6V7K-3XPDX90-4/2/5c3026effc24a7bdb75a3b8ec8c5c78b.*)

El-Naqa, Ali, Al-Momani, Mohammad, Kilani, Suzan, and Hammouri, Nezar, 2007, Groundwater deterioration of shallow groundwater aquifers due to overexploitation in northeast Jordan: CLEAN – Soil, Air, Water. v. 35, p. 156–166. (Also available at *http://onlinelibrary.wiley.com/doi/10.1002/clen.200700012/abstract.*)

Helsel, D.R. and R. M. Hirsch, 2002, Statistical Methods in Water Resources: Techniques of Water Resources Investigations, Book 4, chapter A3, U.S. Geological Survey, 522 p.

Kaudse, T., and Aeschbach-Hertig, W., 2011, Noble gases used as an indicator of groundwater mixing in Azraq, Jordan [abs.]: Proceedings 2011 V.M. Goldschmidt Conference, Prague, p. 1156, accessed November 19, 2012 at *http://goldschmidt.info/2011/abstracts/finalPDFs/1156.pdf.*

Margane, Armin, Hobler, Manfred, Almomani, Mohammad, and Subah, Ali, 2001, Groundwater resources of northern Jordan (v. 4) Contributions to the hydrogeology of northern Jordan: Technical cooperation report, Federal Institute for Geosciences and Natural Resources, and Ministry of Water and Irrigation, Amman, 84 p.

Margane, Armin, Hobler, Manfred, Almomani, Mohammad, and Subah, Ali (eds.), 2002, Contributions to the hydrogeology of northern and central Jordan: Stuttgart, Germany, Schweizerbart Science Publishers, Geologisches Jahrbuch Reihe C, Band C 68, 52 p., ISBN 978-3-510-95890-0.(Also available at *http://www.schweizerbart.de/publications/detail/artno/186046800.*)

Margane, Armin, Borgstedt, Ariane, Subah, Ali, Hajali, Zakkaria, Almomani, Thair, and Hamdan, Ibraheem, 2008, Delineation of surface water protection zones for the Mujib Dam: BGR & MWI Technical Cooperation Project, Groundwater Resources Management, Technical Report No. 10, BGR archive no. 0126002, 132 p., Ministry of Water and Irrigation, Amman.

Margane, Armin, Borgstedt, Ariane, Hamdan, Ibraheem, Subah, Ali, and Hajali, Zakkaria, 2009a, Delineation of surface water protection zones for the Wala Dam: BGR & MWI Technical Cooperation Project, Groundwater Resources Management, Technical Report No. 12, 126 p., Ministry of Water and Irrigation, Amman.

Margane, Armin, Subah, Ali, Hamdan, Ibraheem, Borgstedt, Ariane, Almomani, Thair, Al-Hasani, Ibrahim, Hajali, Zakkaria, Jaber, Ayman, Al-Smadi, Hadeel, and Mamoon, Ismail, 2009b, Delineation of groundwater protection zones for the Hallabat wellfield: BGR & MWI Technical Cooperation Project, Groundwater Resources Management, Technical Report No. 13, 182 p., Ministry of Water and Irrigation, Amman.

Margane, Armin, Subah, Ali, Hamdan, Ibraheem, Almomani, Thair, Hajali, Zakkaria, Ma'moun, Ismail, Al-Hassani, Ibrahim, and Smadi, Hadeel, 2010, Delineation of groundwater protection zones for the Lajjun, Qatrana, Sultani and Ghweir wellfields: BGR & MWI Technical Cooperation Project, Groundwater Resources Management, Technical Report No. 9, 292 p., Ministry of Water and Irrigation, Amman.

Rosenberg, D.E., and Peralta, Richard, 2011, Economic impacts of groundwater drawdown in Jordan: International Resources Group report for U.S. Agency for International Development contract EPP-I-00-04-00024-00, Amman, 29 p.

Salameh, Elias, 1996, Water quality degradation in Jordan (Impacts on Environment, Economy and Future Generations Resources Base): Amman, Jordan, Friedrich Ebert Stiftung, 179 p.

Salameh, Elias, 2004, Using environmental isotopes in the study of the recharge-discharge mechanisms of the Yarmouk catchment area in Jordan: Hydrogeology Journal, v. 12, no. 4, p. 451-463, Doi: 10.1007/s10040-004-0357-x. (Also available at *http://dx.doi.org/10.1007/s10040-004-0357-x.*)

Salameh, Elias, and Bannayan, Helen, 1993, Water resources of Jordan, present status and future potentials: Amman, Jordan, Friedrich Ebert Stiftung, 183 p.

Salameh, E., and El-Naser, H., 2009, Retreat of the Dead Sea and its effect on the surrounding groundwater resources and the stability of its coastal deposits, *in* Hötzl, Heinz, Möller, Peter, and Rosenthal, Eliahu, The water of the Jordan Valley: Berlin, Springer-Verlag, p. 247–264.

Subah, A., Hobler, M., Haj Ali, Z., Khalifa, N., Momani, Th., Atrash, M., Hijazi, H., Ouran, S., Jaber, A., and Tarawneh, R., 2006, Hydrogeological proposal for the delineation of a groundwater protection area for the Wadi Al Arab well field: German-Jordanian Technical Cooperation BGR-Ministry of Water and Irrigation Groundwater Resources Management Technical Report No. 4, PROJECT NO. PN 2001.2132.7, BGR archive no. 0126796, 57 p, Ministry of Water and Irrigation, Amman.

U.S. Agency for International Development, 2010, USAID in Jordan, Water resources management, accessed December 9, 2010 at *http://jordan.usaid.gov/sectors.cfm?inSector=16.*

Appendixes

These appendixes include hydrographs of groundwater levels, graphs of salinity, and trends for all wells analyzed in this study. Click the "Link" to open each appendix.

A – Groundwater Trends in Wells in Azraq Groundwater Basin

[*Link*]

B – Groundwater Trends in Wells in Dead Sea Groundwater Basin

[*Link*]

C – Groundwater Trends in Wells in Hammad Groundwater Basin

[*Link*]

D – Groundwater Trends in Wells in Jordan Side Valleys Groundwater Basin

[*Link*]

E – Groundwater Trends in Wells in Yarmouk Groundwater Basin

[*Link*]

F – Groundwater Trends in Wells in Zarqa Groundwater Basin

[*Link*]

www.ingramcontent.com/pod-product-compliance
Lightning Source LLC
Chambersburg PA
CBHW080427290526
45791CB00008BA/2425